# THE GULL

# THE GULL

## Daphne Marlatt

WITH A JAPANESE TRANSLATION BY TOYOSHI YOSHIHARA

PREFACE BY RICHARD EMMERT

TALONBOOKS

Copyright © 2009 Daphne Marlatt
Translation copyright © 2009 Toyoshi Yoshihara

Talonbooks
P.O. Box 2076, Vancouver, British Columbia, Canada V6B 3S3
www.talonbooks.com

Typeset in Scala and printed and bound in Canada.
Printed on 100% post-consumer recycled paper.

First Printing: 2009

The publisher gratefully acknowledges the financial support of the Canada Council
for the Arts; the Government of Canada through the Book Publishing Industry
Development Program; and the Province of British Columbia through the British
Columbia Arts Council and the Book Publishing Tax Credit for our publishing activ-
ities.

LIBRARY AND ARCHIVES CANADA CATALOGUING IN PUBLICATION

Marlatt, Daphne, 1942–
    The gull / Daphne Marlatt ; with a Japanese translation by Toyoshi
Yoshihara ; preface by Richard Emmert.

A play, winner of the 2008 Uchimura Naoya Prize, in English and Japanese
    translation
ISBN 978-0-88922-616-6

    1. Nō plays. I. Yoshihara, Toyoshi, 1937– II. Title.

PS8576.A74G84 2009          C811'.54          C2009-904786-1

*for the Japanese Canadian fishing families
of Steveston through the years*

# Contents

# Reflections on *The Gull* and English Noh

Richard Emmert

## SOME THOUGHTS ABOUT NOH'S LITERARY CHARACTERISTICS

In the popular 1984 film *Amadeus*, there is a scene where Mozart informs the Austrian Emperor that he wishes to write a German-language opera. To the eighteenth-century Austrian court with its Italian advisors, it was clearly unthinkable to write opera in any language other than Italian. But with Mozart and others, that changed. And as we know now, there are operas performed today written not only in Italian and German, but also in French, English, Japanese and a host of other languages.

Perhaps due to liberal-democratic sensibilities in the present-day West which have led us to think that anything can be written in any language, it does not necessarily seem strange to Westerners that English could be used to write a play in the style of classical Japanese Noh. But to many Japanese versed in Noh, there exist legitimate doubts about this presupposition. While some of them perhaps are of the "it is our tradition—don't mess with it" variety, others are more cognizant of the complexities of

Noh linguistic and narrative structures and their relationship with its music, and the fact that necessarily and together all of these elements are what create a Noh play. It is difficult to create in Japanese. Won't it only be more difficult in English?

To explain all the nuances of these formal interrelationships is certainly not possible in a short essay. But let me try to take on a few of the important ones. To begin with, the Japanese terms for "theatre" and "drama" (*engeki*), or "play" (*shibai*)—all terms that are commonly used in English when referring to Noh—have over the years been studiously avoided in Japanese when describing Noh. "Noh is Noh," people have told me. It is not "theatre" like Western-style realistic drama. Admittedly, in recent years there are writers in Japanese who have begun to include Noh in a broad category of stage arts and quite purposely call it *engeki*—"theatre" or "drama." But that is still not the norm.

Yet, even without considering the Japanese sense of what Noh is, the English terms "theatre," "drama" and "play" are misleading. Noh is a dance drama where elements of highly stylized modes of music, song and dance are prominent and even dialogue is a stylized rendering which is more akin to singing than to speaking. Noh dialogue is delivered with a much more concise and weighty style than "realistic" dialogue. Thus, while any English dialogue could be rendered in Noh style, typical Western-style dialogue plays would be considered far too pompous and boring for the Noh form. Noh typically mixes passages of dialogue with poetic song which, when done well, seem to move the play along, though at a slower pace than would the rhythms and syntax of "realistic" speech. But when Noh poetry has emotional depth, the weight given to its delivery—which includes a sense of space, pause and tension—can create a match of word and sound which is quite powerful and moving to those used to this complex art, and it allows us to witness and feel a range and complexity of human experience and emotion.

There is another tendency in Noh which distinguishes it from typical plays, and that is that plot is not terribly important. Rather than various plot twists and turns presented on stage for the audience to follow as they develop in the fictionalized "real time" of a conventional play, in Noh, actions of the past are presented as completed and emphasis is focused on the moods that are created in the main actor as he or she recalls these incidents. Songs sung by a chorus might describe the scene, or more specifically the thoughts and emotional sensations which the characters are feeling at any given time during a Noh performance.

Thus rather than a realistic play where several characters together move a plot forward, Noh is highly stylized and tends to have one main character whose past story is presented in rich poetic verse generally sung by a chorus whose members are not characters in the play. There is dialogue in which a traveller asks the main character who he/she is, and elicits these stories of the past, the remembrance of which often brings about a dance by the main actor that moves the traveller and the audience to a profound and elemental understanding of the human condition.

While these elements taken together may be quite typical of Noh, there is in fact a great variety of plays in the classical Noh repertory. Still, understanding the parameters of what is possible and why—particularly given the need to make the text work with the music, is something that generally takes reading many Noh plays and seeing enough performances to understand the important relationship that exists in practice between movement, text and music.

## MEETING DAPHNE MARLATT

This preface is really intended to highlight my first meeting with Daphne Marlatt. In August 2003, I went to Vancouver for the first time to give a workshop in the chant and dance of Noh, as well as to begin discussions on the English Noh project which eventually would be called *The Gull*. I had been asked by the producer, Heidi Specht, whose brainchild the project was, to be the composer of its Noh music and co-direct the play with Noh actor Akira Matsui. In previous years, I had already written the music for five English Noh plays and had worked closely with the respective playwrights of a couple of these in shaping the play into a Noh piece. And even though I still have never yet written my own Noh text, I had also begun giving "Writers' Workshops" for playwrights interested in learning about typical Noh structures and perhaps even writing in the style of Japanese classical Noh. This has since become an important annual activity of Theatre Nohgaku, the Noh company I founded in 2000 based in Japan and the United States, dedicated to doing Noh in English.

In any case, I went to Vancouver expecting to encounter a playwright who was used to writing plays using conventional dialogue. Daphne Marlatt was not that. Instead, I found a poet who was already well versed in the large structural characteristics of Noh texts and had both a strong sense of the way her particular play would unfold, as well as an understanding of the importance of limiting a plot in order to enrich it with poetry. What she presented to me in outline form the first night of my arrival in Vancouver was already a clear Noh shaping of her story. From that time on and over the next three years, I helped her understand the specifics of its structure and how it would necessarily affect the music. But the fact that she already "got it" in terms of the big structural issues made our subsequent exchanges that much more creative and interesting for both of us.

## THE FIRST CANADIAN NOH?

Some have called *The Gull* the first Canadian Noh. Over the last several years, I have come across several other writers throughout the world who have clearly been influenced by Noh and have written plays which they call "Noh plays." Some of these texts I have read and they have revealed varying degrees of Noh craft and sensibility. But I have always felt this approach—that a text in and of itself can be a Noh play—reveals a cultural shallowness that does not understand how performance elements combine with text to create a "true" Noh play.

People who tell me they have written a Noh play more often than not are mistakenly thinking that a Noh play is like a Shakespeare play. Shakespeare plays can be done as a Western opera, a kabuki play or a Beijing opera, and all the time still retain their essential identities as Shakespeare plays. But does the reverse work for opera too? For example, we could take the text of Puccini's *La Bohème* and do it as a dialogue play. Would that still be an opera? I think not. Opera is a style in which text is sung: a so-called "operatic style." Similarly, Noh is a style in which text is sung and movement is performed in Noh style. If the same *La Bohème* were done by Noh performers in Noh style, it would likely be termed a Noh performance of a traditional opera text, but it would not be an opera performance of that text. If opera singers sang the classical Noh play *Sumidagawa* in operatic style, they would be true to their profession and be performing an opera; they would not have suddenly become Noh performers.

The point of these ruminations is that Noh, like opera, is a style of performance. If our production of *The Gull* can be labelled the first Canadian Noh, it is because no one has ever previously written a Canadian play that has subsequently been performed in Noh style. The fact that we were able to do precisely that clearly makes our production of *The Gull* a Noh play. And considering there are not many people in Canada performing in the actual Noh style, in terms of movement and music, my guess is that our production was indeed the first Canadian Noh.

My hope is that there will be others.

Richard Emmert is Professor of Asian Theatre, Musashino University, Tokyo; and the Artistic Director and founder of Theatre Nohgaku.

# How *The Gull / Kamome* Took Flight

Daphne Marlatt

## How it Began

When Heidi Specht first called me on the phone in November of 2002 to ask if I would be interested in writing a contemporary Noh play about Steveston for production by Pangaea Arts, two separate currents of longstanding interest suddenly pooled together in my life: Noh and Steveston.

The history of the Japanese Canadian fishing community in Steveston, a fishing village that was once a cannery boom-town at the mouth of the Fraser River, had interested me since 1971 when I happened to walk through Star Camp, the last cannery camp still standing on the riverfront. At that point it had been recently abandoned and was waiting for a bulldozer to clear it away for new development. Those small, empty shacks with thin layers of newsprint for insulation against the sea winds left a strong impression of the impermanence of people's lives at the edge of what had been one of the mightiest salmon rivers in the world. This impression was only a shadow of what must have been the original inhabitants' deep sense of impermanence when, in 1942, the federal government enforced evacuation of Japanese Canadian families from their homes to internment camps a hundred miles from the coast. Restrictions on the movement of Japanese Canadians were not lifted until 1949 when a group of twenty-eight fishermen were allowed back to the coast through negotiation with the UFAWU, the fishermen's union. The canneries soon began urging more to return so in 1950 a much larger number returned and many of them stayed on.

Two years after my walk through Star Camp, I joined an aural history project which, with Maya Koizumi as interviewer and interpreter, recorded the memories of those who had lived through the double uprooting of immigration and wartime internment and then had come back to Steveston. With Maya's translations of those interviews we gradually put together an early book of the community's history called *Steveston Recollected*.[1] While working on that book, Robert Minden and I began putting together a cycle of my poems and his photographs about the village. This book, *Steveston*, was published in 1974 by Talonbooks and was reissued in an enlarged edition by Ronsdale Press in 2001.

The second current, my interest in Noh, began in the early sixties, when I first encountered Noh plays in a course on Japanese literature in translation taught by the eminent critic Dr. Shuichi Kato at the University of British Columbia. Something about the combination of poetry, music and dance, something about the poignancy of the plays themselves with their otherworldly personages, fascinated me. On my first reading tour in Japan in 2000, Bev Curran at Aichi Shukotoku University in Nagoya, asked me what I would like to see and I immediately said Noh. As a result, in Tokyo, Ayako Sato kindly took me to see my first classical Noh and Kyōgen. I was fascinated by the intense concentration of a Noh performance, its meditative stillness even while conveying strong emotion.

So when Heidi called in 2002 I said yes without hesitation even though I knew I was in for a steep learning curve. Heidi had studied Noh movement and chant with Tokyo-based Noh director and musician-composer Richard Emmert and had already discussed what would become known as The Steveston Noh Project with him. With Rick as composer and chorus leader who would train the Canadian cast in movement and chant, the project had clear musical direction. Rick became my invaluable dramaturge and thanks to many conversations with him and his invitation to use his personal Noh library freely while I was visiting him in Tokyo, and thanks also to the first workshop in Noh chant and movement that he taught in Vancouver in September of 2003, I learned much about the musical structure of Noh plays in a relatively short time. What I was learning was intricate and ritualized—it offered scope for poetry to be enacted in a dramatic context.

Heidi wanted the play to feature the historical link between Steveston and Mio, the coastal village in Wakayama from which many of the Steveston fishermen originally emigrated. In the spring of 2004 I travelled to Wakayama, the mountainous prefecture on the Kii Peninsula where Mio is located. In Wakayama City, Rick introduced me to Akira Matsui for the first time. This was an important meeting as Heidi had already told me that she wanted Akira to perform the *shite*, the principal role in the play. I was very much aware of his international stature as a masterful Noh performer of the Kita school and that I was standing in the presence of an Intangible Cultural Asset of Japan, but his vital intensity, his humour and warmth immediately set me at ease. Thanks to the Wakayama City Council's interest in our project, Richard and I were driven out to the fishing village of Mio, known locally as "America-mura," where we visited a hilltop museum dedicated to the emigration of Mio people not to America but to Steveston. There we had the opportunity to talk with Hisakazu Nishihama, the poet-curator of that museum, about picture brides, the young women who emigrated to the new world with only a picture of their husband-to-be to let them know who they would be spending the rest of their lives with. He told us several stories, one of which played a role in my conception of the mother and her background as the daughter of a temple priest. Noh theatre has traditionally been the preserve of male performers, even though many of the plays in the classical repertoire have remarkable roles for women. During our visit to Akira Matsui, watching him unfold some of his richly elegant costumes and show us his masks, watching the grace of all his movements, I realized that he could indeed play the mother role I was beginning to imagine.

Featuring the Mio connection meant that homesickness would be one of the themes of *The Gull*, or *Kamome* in Japanese. But the original spark for the play was something a Nisei fisherman had mentioned during my work in Steveston in the early seventies. He had casually mentioned the ghosts he had seen up the coast when his boat was tied up at what he called China Hat. More research was needed and with the help of Timothy Savage at the Nikkei Centre Museum and the Steveston historian Mitsuo Yesaki, I found myself talking with a small group of retired fishermen who told me that there were two China Hats at different locations on the coast with a number of ghost stories attached to each one. For the purposes of the play, China Hat had to be the First Nations village in Finlayson Channel, now known as Klemtu. Sheltered by a small island shaped like a Chinese farmworker's hat, it was one of the anchorages in the old days when fishermen followed the various runs of salmon along the coast, travelling for several days up to the Skeena River for the early run there and then gradually working their way down the coast for the Fraser River run. The ghost story in *The Gull* is connected to a fishing superstition that says if you see a seagull splashing around in the waves it means a storm is coming.

## WORKING IN THE TRADITION OF NOH THEATRE

To work within the genre of the Noh play is to work within a highly stylized tradition. This is a form of Japanese theatre developed in the fourteenth and fifteenth centuries by two eminent performer-playwrights, Kan'ami and his son Zeami, who not only wrote numerous plays still performed today but also developed the aesthetic involved in acting and writing Noh. Deeply imbued with both Buddhist and Shinto concepts, this theatre fuses music with dance, elaborate costume, mask and poetic script. The music, which is supplied by three different kinds of drums and a specialized flute, forms the basis of the performance. A Noh play is composed of two acts constructed from a series of *shōdan* or brief passages in particular musical modes, each conveying a prescribed segment of the story. For instance, a first act will begin with the *Shidai* or entrance music and song, followed by a prose passage, the *Nanori* or announcement of the name and narrative situation of the *waki* who has come onstage.

Our tradition of realism in Western theatre leads us to have similar expectations of other forms of theatre. Noh theatre,

19

however, is not about plot or character in a realist sense, although it is very much about human passions such as jealousy and longing. In fact, even though the principal roles may be based on historical or legendary people, they are not individualized personalities but figures in a net of relationships torn apart by some traumatic event. The focus is on the nature of the relationship that binds together the *shite* and *waki*. In some passages they even seem to speak for one another, a further remove from realism. Noh works on the level of dream and fate and has much to say about the connection between the mundane and spiritual dimensions of human life.

Music and dance are such integral components of each play, so closely integrated with the gradual unfolding of the story, one could say that the structure of a Noh play is essentially musical and kinetic in slow time. Because each scene is built in a prescribed succession of *shōdan*, each type of which "has a name designating its poetic, musical and kinetic form," as Richard Emmert and Monica Bethe put it so succinctly in their Noh Performance Guides,[2] the climax of a play will be enacted in the major dance performed by the *shite* in Act II. In fact, these elements, dance and music, are as crucial a feature of the play's narrative impact as the words of the script. Noh theatre's sculpting of emotion is multi-sensory and the script alone can only gesture at these other equally significant elements. So the names of the *shōdan* and dances, included in the script, are such gestures. Within the repertoire of Noh, there are distinct names for the narrative functions of various dances and verbal passages, indicative of mood and, often, of the relationship of chanted syllables to drumbeats. The prose passages are not spoken but also chanted in a ritualized style of intonation.

In the script for a Noh play, performers are indicated simply by the generic names for their roles: *shite*, or principal performer; *waki* and *wakitsure*, or main secondary performer and assistant secondary performer; *ji* or chorus; *ai* or *ai-kyōgen*, main performer of the interlude between the two acts. The relationship of the *waki* to the *shite* is that of witness to, and elicitor of, the central actor's story. As emotional relief from the intensity of this dynamic, the *ai* offers more background information on the *shite*'s story and also, in a full Kyōgen play, humour bordering on burlesque, all in a more colloquial style of speech. The *ji* or chorus is not composed of personages but impersonal voices that sometimes sing for the *shite*, sometimes for the *waki*. Traditionally, a day-long festival of Noh plays would present Kyōgen plays (seen as an entirely different form of theatre with independently trained actors) between the Noh plays, thus alternating the tragic and the comic.

Many Noh plays involve the appearance of a restless spirit, someone who has died in an unresolved way. Revealing the deeper meanings of that death comprises the minimalist narrative of the play. In *The Gull*, the *shite* performs the spirit of a woman who came to Steveston from Mio years earlier as a picture bride and who died in the TB sanatorium in New Denver at the end of the internment period. It is a story that stages the suffering of a spirit who, as in life, feels cut off from her original home and cannot free herself from the dichotomies of there or here, then or now, alien or citizen.

## A SYNOPSIS OF THE GULL

Act I. In the summer of 1950, two young Japanese Canadian brothers, in the role of the *waki* and *wakitsure*, return to the coast to fish. These brothers were born in Steveston and the oldest, the *waki*, had gone fishing with his father before the war. Their parents both died during the internment years, so returning to the coast and following their father's old fishing route feels like coming home. With a storm brewing, they take refuge at China Hat. In the dark and rain a creature (the *shite*) appears on the wharf above their boat. One brother sees only a seagull, the other sees a young woman who seems lost. Speaking in Japanese, she tells them she is from Mio and that she came as a picture bride to Steveston years ago. One brother remarks that her story resembles their mother's. She shrieks at them, "Go home," and disappears in the storm.

The Kyōgen Interlude features an older fisherman who turns out to be a friend of their father's. The brothers invite him onboard for more than a few nips of whiskey as the storm increases and the older man starts reminiscing about their mother. The boys tell him about the strange creature they had seen on the wharf. He suggests this may have been their mother's ghost and they should stay up on deck to watch for her return.

Act II. The mother's spirit returns as a middle-aged woman and accuses them of having left her to die far away from Mio and far from the sea. She weeps for her home and the temple where her father was a priest. The brothers mourn her attachment to a Mio that must have changed over the years and they ask her forgiveness. Searching for answers, she dances out her dilemma between Steveston and Mio, here and there. A bell-buoy rings in the wind, she hears the temple bell of Mio and, realizing that one ocean joins both places, she chants the Nembutsu, the refuge mantra of Amitabha Buddha who guides the spirits of the dead to his western paradise. Her spirit finds release and she fades into the early morning calm of the sea.

## How "The Gull" Departs from Classical Noh

As collaborators, Rick and I both felt strongly that we wanted our Canadian play to maintain the traditional musical structure of a Noh play, but the very nature of its story set in 1950 on the West Coast determined certain departures. The first and most obvious departure of the 2006 Pangaea Arts production involved staging a Canadian story written in English and performed as a bicultural collaboration between Japanese and Canadian performers. It was also a partially bilingual production as the lines delivered by Akira Matsui were translated into Japanese by Toyoshi Yoshihara, with a few key words retained in English for the benefit of a largely Anglophone audience. All the other performers were Canadian, rigorously trained by Rick in Noh posture, chant and movement during his visits to Vancouver over the two years leading up to final production. For that production, co-directed by Akira and Rick, Rick led the chorus and blocked some of the Canadian actors' movements onstage while Akira choreographed all the dances as well as some of the actors' movements. All four of the professional Noh musicians came from Japan, two of them women performers—a contemporary development that reflects the advent of women onto the classical stage in Japan.

From the outset, I was not interested in writing a play that would be some kind of fusion between Noh and Western theatre. I wanted *The Gull* to be the transposition of a classical Japanese form into an Canadian mode that would follow the structure of Noh as closely as possible, would create the emotional impact of Noh in its performance, but would tell a story particular to our history. However, there were some serious difficulties in cultural translation. First of all, to use the great Noh theorist Zeami's term, there could be no *honzetsu*, no seed-situation for the play from a well-recognized classical source such as the eleventh-century *Tales of Genji*, or the tenth-century *Tales of Ise*, or to poems from the early classical collections. Noh plays inscribe a wealth of allusion to these and other early literary texts. Canada, as a relatively new nation with a rapidly evolving and changing settler culture, has no equivalent sources of its own. Only in the last fifty years have we even begun to speak of "Canadian classics" of literature. Furthermore, only in the last few decades has the wartime internment of Japanese Canadians entered public consciousness with the accumulating weight of histories, memoirs, novels, photo exhibits, historic sites and even a recent children's opera, thanks to the passionate energies of Japanese Canadian artists and historians committed to fully recording this shameful part of Canadian history.[3]

Secondly, there is the problem of *meisho* or wealth of literary allusions from which to construct the richly textured symbolic associations of a Noh play. The West Coast and particular places along it have a rich and lengthy oral history in the myths of the First Nations peoples who have lived here for thousands of years. But because of the federal government's long attempt to deculturate the indigenous peoples, these are not generally known within the context of Canadian culture at large. In our literature there is little that has been written about the village of Klemtu or the village of Steveston. Neither name registers on the Canadian literary map. Even the names of most coastal features are known only to boaters and fishermen and to native people, not to the general public. Setting the play on a boat tied up at Klemtu/China Hat is a small bow towards that long oral tradition.

Thirdly, *The Gull* does not have the social elevation of many Noh plays involving stories of famous warriors, noblemen who were poets, court ladies and court officials. Its story is about working-class people. This brought a certain element of realism to the production design, integrated as it was with traditional elements. The costumes for the *waki, wakitsure* and *ai* were assembled by our creative costume designer, Margaret McKea, from actual clothes worn by fishermen in the 1950s. On the other hand, she devised the costumes for the *shite* in the elegant classical style of Noh, very much in keeping with the masks carved for the play in traditional style by Wakayama Noh mask-maker Hakuzan Kubo. Furthermore, the musicians all wore traditional costume. Somewhere in between these two poles, the chorus members wore traditional *hakama* (the full, pleated pants that allow for the traditional kneeling posture onstage) along with creatively designed jackets. Instead of the usual symbolic pine tree as backdrop for the stage, we had a scenic backdrop painted from a photograph of the island and that part of the inlet surrounding Klemtu. Set designer Phillip Tidd used imitation wooden pilings for the four pillars that traditionally mark the performance corners of the stage and draped fishing nets with cork floats along the *hashigakari* or bridgeway that is such an important performance component of a Noh stage. So, on the visual level, our production integrated West Coast realism with the classic minimalism of Noh.

In the same way, for the script, the aesthetic qualities of language had to come, not from verbal associations rung on lines from previous classical sources, but from a flow of images arising from its Canadian locale and period. In order to recreate at least a little of the dense intertextuality of Noh plays, I embedded a few lines from poems written by three contemporary Canadian poets, Joy Kogawa, Roy Miki and Roy Kiyooka, as well as a phrase from the well-known Noh play *Sumidagawa*, known in the West because Benjamin Britten used its story for his chamber opera *Curlew River*.

At one point Rick and I had a weekend-long work session during which we went over my draft of Act I and he began setting the words to music. As we sounded the syllables of each line, adding one or two here, cutting one or two there, finding alternate words for those that would be difficult to enunciate clearly in chant, I learned the difference between poetry to be read and poetry to be sung. Unlike Japanese, English is a stressed language, which means that syllables can be drawn out or contracted depending on their meaning. So the alternating seven and five syllable count, set to an eight-beat bar in the *utai* (song) of classical Noh, has to be a little more elastic in English. Furthermore, English tends to be discursive in its sentence structure. I learned that I had to condense what was being said, rely on images to carry verbal associations, and rely on the music of the words in rhyme, off-rhyme and alliteration. Classical Noh plays seem very contemporary in their density of language, particularly in their use of puns and double meaning. So it was a delight to apply a few of these techniques. For instance, the essential pun the play turns on is "gull," the noun for a seabird and the verb for being deceived.

The Kyōgen interlude in *The Gull* is also less traditional in that it stages more dialogue between the *waki* and *wakitsure* and the *ai*. Borrowing from full Kyōgen plays, this interaction is also somewhat comedic in the way the *ai* gulps down his hosts' whiskey while shedding light on the back-story. Throughout *The Gull*, the roles of *waki* and *wakitsure* are more elaborated, the dynamic between the older and younger brother more insistent than in traditional Noh. Given the generational conflict in the play, I felt that it was necessary to have two slightly different takes on the situation in which the brothers find themselves, so it was useful to have a *wakitsure* (attendant to the *waki*) as well as the *waki*.

## REHEARSALS AND FINAL PRODUCTION

Thanks to Simon Johnston's generous support of the project, we began auditioning at the Gateway Theatre in August of 2004 for the Canadian part of the cast: those who would play the roles of *waki, wakitsure* and *ai* and those who would be members of the chorus. All had to be trained from the beginning in Noh posture, movement and chant. They were enthusiastic about this training and Rick, on his way to or from Tokyo, spent many hours in Vancouver working with them. In May of 2005, we held two staged readings without musicians, one in an old cannery now a national heritage site on the wharf in Steveston, and the other at the Nikkei Cultural Centre in Burnaby. Although it was very cold in the cannery site, its wooden plank floor built out over the river with no heat for the audience, both readings drew attentive audiences who gave us verbal and written response to this first experience of *The Gull*. Their comments were much discussed among us and influenced the later stages of costume and set design.

A year elapsed between the staged readings and the full production that took place in May of 2006. Because of this time-lag, we lost one of our actors and one member of our chorus. New auditions were held and the new members of the ensemble had to learn very rapidly. In the end, the Canadian members of the cast featured Vancouver actor Simon Hayama (who grew up in Steveston) as *waki* playing the older brother; Alvin Catacutan from Winnipeg via Los Angeles as *wakitsure* playing the younger brother; Toronto poet and actor David Fujino (who as a child actually experienced the internment years) as *ai* playing the older fisherman; and Ari Solomon, Michael Robinson, Minoru Yamamoto and Kerry VanderGriend, all from Vancouver, as members of the chorus led by Rick. When Akira Matsui arrived, he had already choreographed the *shite* role, but his flexibility led to spontaneous changes and transformations as he directed the movements of the rest of the cast and set his dances within that larger context.

Then the Noh musicians Mitsuo Hama, Hitoshi Sakurai, Naoko Takahashi and Narumi Takizawa joined us from Japan and the actors and chorus started final rehearsals together with the music. Suddenly the play assumed its full shape, a tremendously exciting moment for all of us. By that point, the script was almost complete. I say "almost" because, during the final round of rehearsals, it became clear that the Kyōgen interlude would have to be extended in order to give Akira enough time for his complicated costume change for Act II. I had never written to such instant demand, but after the first moment of panic, I discovered that adding extra exchanges between the brothers about their experience of internment and their mother's death would deepen the emotional impact of the play. As a poet and novelist used to writing alone with my own resources of imagination and research, it was a new step to accommodate the physical requirements of theatre. Through it all, the marvelous enthusiasm, curiosity about Noh and the good humour of the ensemble held us all together under Rick and Akira's expert guidance. Producer and Artistic Director Heidi Specht, whose wild idea this was in the beginning, together with Co-Producer and Project Manager Lenard Stanga, trouble-shooter par excellence, embraced, encouraged and guided us all towards the final goal of production. Despite the many financial and strategic difficulties encountered along the way, Heidi's vision never wavered and *The Gull* took to the boards for six performances in May 2006 on a temporary Noh stage constructed inside a theatre tent on the plaza of Richmond City Hall. This site acknowledged the sponsorship of both Richmond's Gateway Theatre and the city of Richmond in its sister-city relationship to Wakayama City. The calls of actual gulls outside could be heard occasionally as the wind flapped the tent walls in an echo of the play's storm onstage and, as Akira Matsui slowly raised his arms costumed like wings, the gull soared.

WHY NOH?

I have been asked what draws me, a contemporary Canadian poet, to such a strictly traditional form of Japanese theatre? A form which was first developed in the fourteenth century and has not altered during the intervening centuries of performance. How is that form relevant to our time? Asking myself this question prompted two deeper questions that relate to many of the stories of classical Noh: What happens to the mindstream of a woman or a man attached by longing to a place where an intense life-and-death engagement with another was enacted, either through hatred or through love? How does this attachment keep one tied to the memory of that long-gone person or that long-ago place, even though everything else has moved on? The poignancy of Noh's enactments of impermanence as we enter a period of accelerated change is, I think, very relevant today. Furthermore, certain Noh plays, the god plays, recreate the presence of the sacred onstage. That which is sacred appears out of that which has seemed mundane and perfectly ordinary. Now, if we change "sacred" to "other-worldly," this can be said of most Noh plays, many of which exhibit a profound interest in dream, in haunting, in life beyond death. The folding-together of these two levels of reality, the sacred or other-worldly and the mundane, enlarges our view of what we live within, releases us from a narrow focus on, an obsession even, with the materiality of our everyday life and the market-driven pace of the world we live in.

I love the intense focus of Noh, its meditative stillness as background for deliberate movement. How focused they are, the performers and the *hayashi* (musicians) and *ji* (chorus), sitting eyes downcast and deeply still as if in meditation when not singing or playing, deliberate in their pacing and movements when they are performing. Inner focus, maintained throughout the performance by all performers, is a hallmark of good Noh. For an observer, there is a paradox here, the paradox of a restrained, already prescribed spectacle being slowly enacted on stage while creating, at the same time, a vivid sense of inner engagement in the audience. This engagement is produced largely through the mastery of internal concentration and projection of emotion by the *shite* first of all, even through a wooden mask, even while dancing, and by the *waki* and *wakitsure* as witnesses to the *shite*'s story. Intensity is further created by the interlocking patterns of the music and the drummers' calls (*kakegoe*) and the rising and falling of lines chanted by the chorus.

Karen Brazell calls the style in which many Noh plays are written "stream-of-imagery style,"[4] a term that can be read as a play on the "stream of consciousness" style of modernist fiction in the West. Because the text is conveyed in images, a Noh play can powerfully translate psychological conflict into a series of repeating images that verbally re-enact the obsessive nature of this conflict. Noh re-enacts attachment to lovers who are transient, to enmities long-played-out, to bodies that have withered and died, to places that have become nearly unrecognizable over the years, and it conveys the emotional truth of how this attachment amounts to a haunting that is a form of intense suffering. The play in its unfolding works as a ritual release from that suffering.

With such emotional depth, combined with the spectacular quality of dance, of costumes, masks and fans in ritual slow movement, as well as the intensity of drumming and the peculiarly haunting quality of a Noh flute, together with the chanting of a life-story unfolding through a dense weave of intertextual imagery, how could Noh fail to attract a poet? Thanks to outstanding performances by Akira Matsui and the whole ensemble, thanks to the in-depth training that Rick and Akira gave the Canadian cast, and thanks to terrific staging in all aspects, *The Gull* lived up to the dramatically lyric potential that Noh theatre offers.

## NOTES

1. This was published by the Aural History Division of the Provincial Archives of British Columbia as *Steveston Recollected: A Japanese-Canadian History*, edited by Daphne Marlatt, interviews and translations by Maya Koizumi, contemporary photographs by Robert Minden and Rex Weyler.

2. See Noh Performance Guide 1, *Matsukaze*, by Richard Emmert and Monica Bethe, with translation by Royall Tyler (Tokyo: National Noh Theatre, 1992), p. 4.

3. See, for instance, Shizuye Takashima, *A Child in Prison Camp* (1972); Joy Kogawa, *Obasan* (1981), *Itsuka* (1992) and *Naomi's Road* (1986); Muriel Kitagawa, *This is My Own: Letters to Wes and Other Writings 1941–1948* (1985) edited by Roy Miki; Roy Miki and Cassandra Kobayashi, *Justice in Our Time: The Japanese Canadian Redress Settlement* (1991); and Roy Miki, *Redress: Inside the Japanese Canadian Call for Justice* (2004).

4. Karen Brazell, *Traditional Japanese Theater* (New York: Columbia University Press, 1998), p. 144.

# Acknowledgements

Heartfelt thanks to my dramaturge, Richard Emmert, who taught me so much about the structure of Noh—this play could not have been written without him—and to Akira Matsui, who continuously imparted the spirit of Noh; to Heidi Specht for her inspiration and unwavering faith in the project, and to all the truly dedicated performers for bringing *The Gull* to life.

My thanks to Toyoshi Yoshihara for his inspired translation of the play; to Lenard Stanga for can-do energy and an unfailing sense of humour during rehearsal and production; to the designers, Margaret McKea, Phillip Tidd and Bill Davey for their creativity.

My gratitude to the poets who allowed their lines to be woven into *The Gull*: Roy Miki for lines from his "Sansei Poem" quoted in Act I, from *Saving Face* (Winnipeg: Turnstone Press, 1991); Joy Kogawa for lines from "Open Marriage" quoted in Act I, from *A Garden of Anchors: Selected Poems* (Oakville: Mosaic Press, 2003); and Roy Kiyooka, with permission from Kiyo Kiyooka, literary executor for his estate, for lines quoted in Act II from "Wheels," in variant editions, *Pacific Windows*, ed. Roy Miki (Vancouver: Talonbooks, 1997) and *Paper Doors: An Anthology of Japanese-*

*Canadian Literature*, ed. Gerry Shikatani, David Aylward (Toronto: Coach House Press, 1981).

Grateful thanks to the B.C. Arts Council for a writing grant and financial assistance for my research trip to Japan. Many thanks also to the following: Jim Kojima and the Richmond City Council; Dr. N. Iwahashi for the visit to Mio; Mayor Kenichi Ohashi and members of the of the Wakayama City Council; Yoshiko Kitagawa (Wakayama City) for her hospitality; Hisakazu Nishihama of the Mio Museum; Bev Curran (Nagoya); Simon Johnston (Gateway Theatre); Timothy Savage (Nikkei Centre Museum) and Saki Nishimura, Moe Yesaki, Paul Kariya, Ken Takahashi, Frank Kanno, Toshio Murao, Hayao Sakai, Robert Johnston, Ellen Enomoto and Judy Specht for help with research on this coast; Susie Roote for the photograph of China Hat.

With much appreciation to Karl and Christy Siegler for their expert editing and to Talonbooks for producing this beautiful bilingual edition of *The Gull*.

# THE GULL

*The Gull* was produced by Pangaea Arts May 10–14, 2006 as "The Steveston Noh Project," a theatre collaboration between Canadian actors and Noh performers from Japan, with music by Richard Emmert. The play was staged in a theatre tent erected on the plaza of Richmond City Hall, a suburb of Vancouver that incorporates the village of Steveston.

## CAST:

| | |
|---|---|
| SHITE, the gull/mother, a ghost | Akira Matsui |
| WAKI, Canadian-born fisherman | Simon Hayama |
| WAKITSURE, younger brother to the *waki* | Alvin Catacutan |
| AI-KYŌGEN, older Japanese Canadian fisherman | David Fujino |

JI (or Chorus), led by Richard Emmert

Ari Solomon
Michael Robinson
Minoru Yamamoto
Kerry VanderGriend

## MUSICIANS:

| | |
|---|---|
| *Ōtsuzumi* (hip drum) | Mitsuo Kama |
| *Kotsuzumi* (shoulder drum) | Naoko Takahashi |
| *Taiko* (stick drum) | Hitoshi Sakurai |
| *Nōkan* (Noh flute) | Narumi Takizawa |

| | |
|---|---|
| Producer, Artistic Director | Heidi Specht |
| Producer, Project Manager | Lenard Stanga |
| Director, Choreographer | Akira Matsui |

# Maeba (Act I)

## 1

Shidai *(entrance music) for* WAKI *and* WAKITSURE *who walk down bridgeway to main stage, one carrying a lantern and the other a net slung over his shoulder and a gaff.*

### SHIDAI
(*entrance song*)

WAKI/WAKITSURE:
    in late spring's drenching sea-mist we return at last
    in late spring's drenching sea-mist we return at last
    to fish the grounds our father knew, this wild spray

JI (*Chorus*):
    in late spring's drenching sea-mist we return at last
    to fish the grounds our father knew, this wild spray—

## NANORI
### (*name announcement*)

WAKI *and* WAKITSURE *now on stage face front.*

WAKI:

We are *nisei* fishermen heading up the coast from
Steveston. Five years after the war ended, eight years
after we were exiled from this coast where we were born,
we have finally been allowed back to fish. We brothers
are fishing for a Steveston cannery, although we no
longer have our father's boat. Our parents died in the
mountains where we were interned after everything we
had was seized and sold. Now we have come back. On a
rented boat we are heading up the coast for the Skeena
run.

## MICHIYUKI
### (*travel song*)

WAKI/WAKITSURE:

through channels we remember
Seymour Narrows, Ripple Rock
tides, old landmarks

*Uchikiri (brief instrumental break).*

WAKITSURE:

Seymour Narrows, Ripple Rock
tides, old landmarks

WAKI/WAKITSURE:

> spar buoys, bell buoys, "white ladies"—
> then Johnstone Strait where
> pods of killer whales leap up
> greeting our return—

*Uchikiri.*

> trapped in mountains
> we thought we'd never again
> steady the wheel
> as the boat bucks in a swell
> rolling in rough sea now
> Queen Charlotte Sound, its dolphin crests
> for miles we push north
> to Milbanke, hugging Swindle's shore
> we cheat the rising wind
>
> and there, out of the dusk
> in last light, that rocky cone—
> looming in last light that rocky cone.

## TSUKI-ZERIFU
### (*arrival announcement*)

WAKI:

> (*facing front*) We have reached China Hat. Its rocky shape
> offers refuge from a building storm. We will tie up here
> beside other boats from Steveston and ride out the night.
> Like homing salmon we have returned to this small bay.

## 2

Issei *(entrance music)* MAEJITE *(SHITE of Act I) enters bridgeway as gull-woman, wearing a young woman mask and dressed in pale kimono under gauzy cloak.*

### ISSEI
#### (SHITE *entrance song*)

SHITE *(in Japanese)*:
>     lost bird caught in history's torrent
>     having no home to call my own, no refuge in
>     the battering waves that come and come

### SASHI
#### (*recitation, sung*)

SHITE *(in Japanese)*:
>     lulled by the promise of a good life
>     hapless gull I came looking

SHITE *remains motionless on bridgeway while* JI *sings for her.*

JI:
>     blown off-course by karmic winds
>     gulled I was, far from home
>     in a wild estuary and its dream

## UTA
*(song with lines from a contemporary poem)*

Jı:

> *once    we said*
> *we say    the world lay*
> *a mixture    the sun*
> *the sea    our children*
> *like marigolds    our boats*
> *our nets    we*
> *filled our houses*

> in the dream that strands

## Jö-No-Eı
*(high-pitched poem)*

Sʜɪᴛᴇ *(in Japanese)*:
> fury drives me as waves mount
> wretched bird that I am

> Sʜɪᴛᴇ *covers her face with cloak and sits on bridgeway.*

Jı:

> should anyone ask, I am not at home
> here where destiny's rough wind
> has stranded me

# 3

## MONDO
(*prose dialogue*)

WAKI (*rising with* WAKITSURE):
Who is that talking on the wharf in all this rain?

WAKITSURE:
I don't hear anyone. Just a gull calling.

WAKI:
It sounds like a woman. But who in this Indian village would be speaking Nihongo? (*turns to* SHITE) Pardon me, but were you speaking to us?

SHITE *turns away.*

WAKITSURE:
Strange bird. Tucking its head under a wing.

WAKI:
Can't you see she's a woman? She's hiding her face in the fold of her sleeve. Perhaps we startled her.

WAKITSURE (*lifting lantern*):
Hard to see in the dark and the rain.

WAKI:

> Woman or gull, let's see if she will speak to us. Hello—
> *Konbanwa*. We don't mean to frighten you. Where are
> you from?

SHITE (*lifts her head and turns slowly to face* WAKI
*speaking/singing a mixture of Japanese and English, keeping
underlined words in English*):

> Birds of passage come and go but my <u>home</u>—my home
> wah, Mio desu—my only <u>home</u> is Mio.

WAKI:

> Did you say Mio? Mio in Wakayama? Why, that was our
> mother's village—ha ha no village-desu. What is your
> family name?

SHITE (*addressing them in Japanese and some English*):

> Alone I ride the waves of this coast, having no <u>child</u>, no
> <u>husband</u>, no <u>father</u>, no <u>mother</u>.

WAKITSURE:

> What is she saying?

WAKI (*to* WAKITSURE):

> Listening to her is like listening to our mother—I
> understand only part of her *Nihongo*. I think she says she
> has no family, that she is lost somehow.

SHITE (*in Japanese*):

> Spirit flies like a gull and yet, and yet, I am stuck.

WAKI (*addressing* SHITE):

> We were born on this coast and our father sent us to public school in English. Please forgive my broken *Nihongo*.

SHITE (*in Japanese*):

> Ah, poor Mio birds, splashing along an alien shore.

WAKI:

> You, a young woman newly arrived from Wakayama, how did you come to this faraway inlet, this Indian village?

SHITE (*classical lines sung in Japanese*):

> *Ware mo mata*
> *Iza koto towan miyako-dori*\*
>
> —anguished words from an old play you would not understand. Poor Mio birds, you know nothing of <u>home</u>.

WAKI:

> Home, you say? This salmon-coast is our home. And we fishermen are glad to be free now to return.

SHITE:

> Mio birds—<u>Mio</u> "<u>bahdo</u>"—blown far off-course. Can you not see what happens here?

> SHITE *kneels.*

---

\* "I in turn ask you the question, Miyako birds ... " In these lines from the Noh play *Sumidagawa*, the question addressed to the gulls is whether the mother's lost son is dead or alive.

## UTA
*(song with lines from a contemporary poem)*

JI:

under wharf-lights
our *shadows fade and grow*
*back to front, short to long*
our faces don't fit the
language we speak
*constantly checking, these*
*freedom-heavy days*

such is the story of freedom on this coast
an old old story I've seen played out

## MONDO
*(prose dialogue)*

WAKI (*to* WAKITSURE):

Strange. What she says sounds very familiar.

TSURE:

What do you mean?

WAKI:

It sounds like something our mother would say when
she was homesick for Mio.

TSURE:

You mean when she wanted to go back after the war?

WAKI:

No, even earlier—but you were too young to remember.

WAKITSURE *sits.* WAKI *moves to centre stage.*

# 4

## KURI
*(sung poem, rhythm not matched with drum beats)*

JI *(singing for* WAKI):

years ago, a bride she came across the sea
leaving the boats of Mio, her parents' temple home
leaving a prayer at the Dragon-God Shrine
at Kobe she said goodbye

## SASHI
*(recitation, sung)*

WAKI:

passing Cape Hinomisaki

JI:

with wet sleeves
she turned from the headland she knew,
gazing instead at the promise
held in her hand,
a small photo of her husband-to-be

WAKI:

young, firm of body

JI:

and the words he sent
a river teeming with fish, at its mouth
a village newly-built, wide-open sky—

WAKI:

    a future for her shining there

SHITE (*in Japanese*):

    I saw my future shining just ahead

    SHITE *slips off cloak and rises.*

JI:

    she saw her future shining there

## KUSE

(*core narrative, song matched with drum beats accompanied by*
SHITE *dance*)

    SHITE *stands on bridgeway, raising sleeve-wings, moves onstage
and begins to dance slowly, then speeds up after she sings her
single line below.*

JI:

    only a dream as things turned out
    he was older than his photo, and the place itself
    a wild estuary the winter winds keened through
    thin walls of TB huts,
    the strikes, the babies,
    debt an endless round he pulled us from
    to own his boat, his net, his home at last

    *Uchikiri as* SHITE *dances.*

but there were taunts and threats
and then the war—
they took our boats, our homes
our cars we'd worked so hard for
—all lost, seized and sold
to pay for our keep as "enemy
aliens"—condemned,
families split and sent
from the coast to camps far away,
in icy crowded huts and ghost
town rooms we were penned up
in the frozen mountains.

SHITE (*in Japanese*):
fury scalds my wings remembering

JI:

how gulled we were, her cry
her splash in the spray of China Hat's
seething storm—

*During the following,* SHITE *moves to bridgeway, turns to face
standing* WAKI *and* WAKITSURE, *swoops towards them, turns
again, and moves down bridgeway.*

JI:

strange, her story resembles our mother's
—wait, he calls, who are you?
as she lifts drenched wings torn
ragged in the round of migration
only a gull's shriek beats the air—

    fool Mio-birds,
    go home! go home!

*On the last line* SHITE *raises a "wing." Brief and piercing
Nōkan flute solo as* SHITE *exits rapidly.*

JI:

    mirage of the wind, rain fury,
    no woman after all, but a gull, a gull
    yet she did speak.

# Kyōgen Interlude

## 5

*A1 enters and walks down bridgeway singing first verse of folk*
*song, "Kushimoto Bushi."*

A1:

> *Hi no no misaki ni todai aredo*
> *Koi no yamiji wa tera syaseenu*
> *Ara yoisho yoisho yoisho yoisho yoisho*

A1 (*at shite-pillar*):

> I am a *nikkei* fisherman. Once I was based in Steveston,
> and then in the mountains in Kaslo—not much fishing
> in Kaslo. Last year I returned to the coast, one of the first
> to come back after restrictions were lifted. This year I see
> there are more of us tied up here at China Hat. (*turns to*
> WAKI *and* WAKITSURE) Here's a late-comer. Ho there!
> Looks like you made it just in time.

WAKITSURE:

> Someone's hailing us from the wharf—an older fisherman.

WAKI (*rising with* WAKITSURE):

> Hello! There's a storm on the way. Come aboard!

AI (*moving toward them*):

> Storm be damned! It's a fine thing to see more of us back on the coast. Still, you'd better keep an eye on your gear when you're tied up—you've probably figured that out by now. Who are you guys fishing for?

WAKI:

> We're fishing for Nelson Brothers.

AI:

> You must be Arakawa's sons.

WAKI:

> You knew him?

AI:

> Knew him! We fished the Skeena together for many seasons. I remember the summer of '41 when he had his oldest boy with him. That must be you, right? I'm Harry Takahashi.

WAKI:

> Takahashi-san! It's been nine long years. I didn't recognize you.

AI:

Ah, too much has happened in those years. The Coast is still the same but we are not. I was with your father at the road camp in the Rockies but then they shipped me off to another one. That's where I heard about his accident. He was a good fisherman, one of the best. He'd be proud as hell to see you boys back at it.

WAKI:

It's so good to see you again. Let's celebrate.

AI:

A shot of whiskey would warm us up in all this rain.

WAKITSURE:

It would indeed. Please have a seat. (*Sets seat under* AI, *brings mugs to both men and bottle.*) Let me pour for you. (*Pours for each in turn.*)

AI:

*Kampai.* (*both drink*) Ahh! I won't stay long—the wind's picking up. Tell me, how is your mother?

*Sharp ōtsuzumi drum roll.*

WAKITSURE (*staggers*):
Ho, THAT was a wave!

WAKI (*rocking briefly along with* AI):
Our mother passed away in the TB sanatorium in New Denver soon after the war ended.

AI:

> I'm sorry to hear it. Both your parents gone.

WAKI:

> She was most unhappy. She wanted us to sign up for what they called repatriation. She'd had enough, she said.

AI (*shaking his head*):

> Ah, your mother! (*indicates that his mug is empty*)

WAKITSURE:

> How about another shot? (AI *lifts his mug,* WAKITSURE *pours again.*)

AI:

> Aaah! (*smacking his lips*) Your mother now, she was quite a woman. She had that old Wakayama spirit. What a catch! I used to kid your dad about being a highliner in more ways than one.

> *Sharp ōtsuzumi drum roll.*

WAKITSURE (*rocking as the others do too in another "wave"*):

> Hey, it's getting rough!

AI:

> We must be in for a big one. There was a gull splashing around in the waves. When you see that you know bad weather's coming.

WAKI:

So you saw it too?

WAKITSURE:

Just before you came, we heard this gull talking on the wharf. It seemed to be scolding us.

AI:

Gulls sound like that. You boys have spent too long in the mountains. (*holding out his mug for more whiskey which* WAKITSURE *pours*)

WAKI:

This was no ordinary gull, Takahashi-san. It spoke. I know it sounds crazy but it spoke to us in Japanese. It said we should go home.

AI (*with a chuckle*):

So even the gulls are telling us to go "home"?

*Sharp ōtsuzumi drum roll.*

AI, WAKITSURE AND WAKI:

(*all rock in another "wave"*) Whoah!

WAKI:

No. I think she meant we'd come to the wrong place.

AI:

She, you say? Hmm. Perhaps what you saw wasn't a gull. There are stories about China Hat, you know. Some men say they have seen ghosts on their boats.

WAKI *and* WAKITSURE *look at each other.*

WAKI:

I wonder ... (*to* AI): You were going to tell us more about our mother?

AI:

*Ah so ka*! I remember when she first arrived, I thought your Dad did mighty well sending a younger photo of himself to Mio. A lot of fellows did that then. They weren't sure a woman would come all the way across the ocean if she saw them as they really were. She was some fifteen years younger, daughter of the priest in the temple at Mio as I recall. She had some education, she was good-looking—no doubt she could have made a better marriage. But she had an adventurous spirit, she wanted to see the world. Steveston wasn't at all what she expected. Such a wild river, she would say whenever it flooded. Fires and floods, cannery shacks on pilings, one little tap at the end of the boardwalk. She complained but she worked hard, raised you kids, did her time in the cannery like so many wives. You could tell she'd imagined some other life for herself. Your dad once told me that he'd agreed to go back to Wakayama once he made enough money. But he liked it here. So of course the money went into a boat, and then into their own house, and then into a new boat. Fishing got tougher and tougher. And then the war ...

WAKI:

Yes, the war ... it was a very hard time.

AI:

> You were still boys then. You were sent to Orchard with your mother?

WAKI:

> First we went to Greenwood with other families from Steveston.

WAKITSURE:

> They put us up in an old hotel that had been closed down. We were crowded together, all sharing one kitchen.

WAKI:

> But we were lucky. We heard later that people in Popoff had only tents that first winter. In the morning there would be frost on their blankets.

AI:

> *So da da.* We were moved from the road camp to Slocan to build shacks for everyone but we couldn't get them built fast enough before winter set in.

WAKITSURE:

> I remember the winter when a care package came from Japan. There was *sencha* in it and Mother made tea for everyone. She took such small sips trying to make it last. This is the taste of home, she told us.

AI:

> Ah, *sencha*! What can beat good *sencha*? Whiskey perhaps ... (*He signals to the* WAKITSURE *who pours for him.* WAKI *declines.*)

WAKI:

> By that time she was coughing badly.

AI:

> I remember that little cough of hers!

WAKI:

> It got worse in Greenwood. She was coughing blood.

WAKITSURE:

> That's when they moved us to Orchard. Some people had left for the beet farms so there was space.

WAKI:

> Yes, the repatriation order had come down. She said we should leave, we should go to Mio. Father had died in the road camp and she thought that life would be too difficult here without him.

WAKITSURE:

> But we told her we could get jobs. They wanted men in the logging camps.

WAKI:

> In any case, she was too sick to make the journey.

WAKITSURE:

> She said Canada didn't want us.

AI:

> Well, there are *hakujin* who feel that way. As you know.

WAKI:

> But Takahashi-san. We were born here, we can't speak Japanese—Steveston is home to us.

AI:

> It's difficult for your generation. Not Japanese—not Canadian. She died in the sanatorium?

WAKI:

> Yes. We were away logging when we heard she was dying. We got back as soon as we could. She was lying in a ward. They drew the curtains around us but she was trying so hard to breathe. She kept asking for the sea, for a wind ...

*Sharp ōtsuzumi drum roll.*

WAKI, AI AND WAKITSURE (*almost rocked off their seats*):
Hey!

AI:

> That's some wave! I'd better be getting back to my boat. (*moves to stage right, peers out, turns back*) Strange. It's clearing up out there, not much of a storm after all.

WAKI:

So what has been rocking our boat?

AI:

Ah, that must be something else. (*pause*) That "gull," whatever you saw—who knows? Perhaps it was your mother's troubled spirit.

WAKITSURE:

But how would she find us here?

AI:

China Hat is a strange place. It seems to attract spirits.

WAKI:

So what should we do?

AI:

I think you boys should hang around on deck. Maybe that gull-spirit wants to tell you something.

WAKI:

Could it be our mother? (*turning to* AI) We will wait up and see. Thank you for your help.

AI *walks slowly to bridgeway, stops partway down it, looks up at the sky, looks out to sea, then turns back to the* WAKI *and* WAKITSURE *who are watching him. He nods. They bow in respect. He walks down the rest of the bridgeway singing the last few lines of the song quietly to himself.*

# Nochiba (Act II)

## 6

### MACHIUTAI
(*waiting song*)

WAKI/WAKITSURE:
> wrapped in an old blanket
> against the wind, storm abating
> we doze on deck

*Uchikiri, brief instrumental break.*

> against the wind, storm abating
> we doze on deck
> waiting for her troubled spirit
> caught between both worlds
> rocking our boat and our will
> to return to this coast—
> will she appear again, even in dream?
> will she appear in a dream?

# 7

Deha *(music for appearance of ghost) as* NOCHIJITE *(*SHITE *of Act II) begins to appear, wearing mask of a middle-aged woman and traditional kimono. She is half-hidden by the bridgeway entrance curtain.*

### ISSEI/SASHI
*(song not matched to drum beats, recitation)*

SHITE *(in Japanese):*
>between death and birth I hover
>only my own lost face in the stormy
>waves of return

SHITE *comes into full view on bridgeway and walks down to shite pillar onstage.*

JI:
>condemned forever to fly on the dark
>side of the sea my voice cries piteously
>above the waves to you who say
>you have settled here

# 8

## Kake-Ai
### (*sung exchange*)

Waki (*rising*):
> She is here on our deck, dim in the moon's light barred
> by clouds.

Wakitsure (*also rises*):
> So quickly the cloud-bars shift. I see a form glimmering
> there. Can that be you, Mother?

Shite (*in Japanese except for underlined words*):
> <u>My</u> <u>sons</u>, do you recognize this lost one?

Waki (*to* Wakitsure):
> She is not in a form we can touch.

Shite (*in Japanese*):
> On the dark side of the sea ...

Wakitsure:
> Are you really here, Mother?

> Wakitsure *starts to move toward* Shite, *but is held back by*
> Waki's *outstretched arm.*

Shite:
> Not on this side of the sea.

WAKI (*to* WAKITSURE):
> Not here—on the other side ...

SHITE (*in Japanese and English*):
> On the other side of the sea is Mio, my lost <u>home</u>.

### DAN-UTA
#### (*scene song by* JI)

SHITE *mime-dances.*

JI:
> on the far shore of endless ocean
> where surf beats the pine-fragrant Kii
> the small bay where centuries-long
> shirasu nets were hauled up to dry
> and I pulled the bell-rope
> in my father's temple, chanting
> Namu Amida Butsu, Amida Bu—who guides
> the lost through stormy waves to his Western
> Paradise, Amida who alone can cut
> the cord of attachment, o to pull
> that bell again, o the ache
> of this pull back to Mio

# 9

## KAKE-AI
### (*sung exchange*)

WAKI (*rising with* WAKITSURE):
>    but Mio is changed now
>    as we were changed
>    by gale-force winds of war

>    SHITE *turns back to bridgeway.*

JI:

>    poor suffering bird
>    caught in the storm of your own
>    longing for what was

SHITE (*in English*):
>    you, my sons—

JI:

>    —my sons, born from me
>    can you not see what
>    matters most?—home, the nesting ground

WAKI:

>    Mother, your distress
>    saddens us, for where on earth
>    is there a place unchanged
>    by the shifty winds of time?

WAKITSURE:
>even here
>you see how strong the waves of change—
>how they confound us—

SHITE:
>O this cord tangling my feet,

JI:
>this bitterness still—
>so tightly it binds my
>wandering spirit.

Iroe *(musical passage)*.

SHITE *circles stage, coming to a stop in front of her sons whom she accuses.*

## 10

### Ei
### (*poem*)

SHITE (*in English*):
you let me die—

JI:

you let me die
locked away in a mountain hospital
no breath left, no sea-wind
to lift me home

WAKI:

Mother, we failed to understand
how deeply you felt
abandoned there—

WAKI, WAKITSURE:
forgive our blindness.

SHITE (*in English*):
home—you must go!

WAKI:

what was home to you
Mother, is not home to us.

SHITE *moves away in despair as* JI *sings.*

JI:

> home, it changes like the sea's
> rough waves we ride
> its changes constant, changing
> our quick lives—

WAKI *and* WAKITSURE *sit as* SHITE *circles stage in her
anguish while* JI *chants* Noriji.

## NORIJI
*(song in matched rhythm, one syllable per beat)*

JI:

> caught, she turns this way and that,
> desperate to understand
> what they are saying—wave? change?
>
> *nothing but a mouthful of syllables
> to posit an ocean's breath*, the poet wrote
> *nothing but brine and a little bite of air—*

## EI
*(poem)*

SHITE *begins slow dance,* Dan-No-Jo, *as chorus sings poem.*

JI:

> salt wind, heart's breath
> blows quick, blows for miles

SHITE *moves into* Hayamai, *quick dance.*

## 11

### KIRI
#### (*sung conclusion*)

SHITE (*in Japanese*):
ocean singing ocean's breath

JI:

ocean singing ocean's breath
a living tide of syllables
to wash out the line that divides
shore from shore in her
anguished mind—

SHITE (*turning from side to side*):
Canada no kishi-ka?
Kii no hama?

JI:

that Wakayama village there?
this Canada coast here?

then through her storm a bell-buoy sounds
tossed by waves, a temple bell
she hears and turning sees
ocean joining here and there
one current circles through
torrents of disparate naming
wave on wave—

SHITE *stops dancing, listens.*

JI:

in a lull we hear the name so faint
Amida Butsu
tossed by the waves
Amida Butsu
ringing China Hat and Hinomisaki
Namu Amida Butsu, Amida Butsu
in one breath, one precious
human breath to join their
emptiness, her understanding
quick as a bird, her
release—

SHITE *turns to look at the brothers, then moves toward the bridgeway, arms lifted and exits quickly.*

WAKI *comes to stage front and looks towards where she has disappeared.*

JI:

as dawn's early glimmer
brings to light the bay
her mind, released from anguish
fades in bliss, a calm
unbroken sea, one last
murmur a wave
fading to
calm unbroken sea

**Top**: The musicians (*hayashi*) (L–R): Hitoshi Sakurai on taiko drum, Mitsuo Kama on ōtsuzumi drum, Naoko Takahashi on kotsuzumi drum and Narumi Takizawa on nōkan (flute).

**Bottom**: The chorus (*ji*) (L–R): Ari Solomon, Michael Robinson, Richard Emmert, Minoru Yamamoto, Kerry VanderGriend. *Photos by Michael Ford.*

**Above**: Simon Hayama as *waki*, lifting his lantern to see the gull-woman in Act I.
*Photo by Michael Ford.*

# THE GULL

# かもめ

ダフネ・マーラット　作

吉原豊司　訳

「かもめ」――ダフネ・マーラットによる
日系カナダ人をテーマにした英語能 (二〇〇六)

リチャード・エマート

## 解　題

「かもめ (The Gull)」は女流詩人ダフネ・マーラット (Daphne Marlatt) 氏の原作・脚本によるもので、カナダで作られた初の英語能ということができます。初演は、二〇〇六年五月、カナダ西海岸、バンクーバーに隣接するリッチモンド市・市役所前の巨大仮設テントの中に能舞台を組んで上演されました。企画・主催はバンクーバーの劇団パンゲア・アーツです。日本から参加した喜多流シテ方松井彬氏と私、エマートが共同演出に当たり、松井氏は型付け、そしてシテの役を勤め、私は作曲・音楽監督をかねて地頭を勤めました。囃子方も日本からで、一噌流笛を稽古する滝沢成美氏、同じく大倉流小鼓の高橋奈王子氏、同じく葛野流大鼓の釜三夫氏、そして特に金春流太鼓方の桜井均氏の参加を得ました。

かもめ

# 能の要約

この「かもめ」の構造は能の代表的な二場構成の夢幻能形式です。日系カナダ人が強制収容所から解放された戦後の話で、場所はカナダ西海岸。時は一九五〇年夏。前場は若い漁師の二人兄弟がワキ・ワキツレとして船でサケ漁に出かける道行に始まります。この兄弟はスティーブストン村（現在リチモンド市内）出身の日系人で、収容所に拘留中、両親を亡くしました。父がやっていた漁師の仕事は、戦後しばらく日系人には許されなかったのが、五年たってやっと許され、兄弟は父の跡を継いで借りた船でサケ漁に出ることができました。そこの桟橋に不思議な女性（シテ）が現れます。弟はカモメだと言うが、兄は明かすことにします。ある晩、時化に遭い、チャイナハットという波止場で一夜を母に似て英語混じり日本語を喋る女性だと言います。すると、この女・カモメは「私は和歌山の三尾から写真花嫁でカナダに来た」と言うので、まさに亡くなった母の人生と同様に兄弟は思いました。血その女・カモメがついに三尾に帰ることができなかった悲しい人生を語り、そして兄弟に向かい、の故郷である日本の『ホームへ帰れ』と言ってカモメのように飛んで消えます。

間狂言の年老いた日系漁師が、兄弟の船にやってきて、突然、時化の影響でもないのに船が大きく揺れます。老漁師はチャイ両親の昔話をしているうちに、ナハットはよく亡霊が現れるところだと言い、兄弟が見たカモメはもしかすると、成仏できないでいる彼らの母の霊ではないかと告げます。

後場は、船のデッキでまどろむ兄弟の夢の中に、母の霊が本当の姿で現れます。自らの苦難と、故郷の和歌山の三尾への執着や思慕、そして故郷に帰れないままカナダの山奥の病院に閉じ込められて死んだ、その恨みを語ります。兄弟は母に、彼らにとっての故郷は母と違って、海のように変わりゆ

3

くものだと言います。それは、苦労した母の霊には理解し難いことでしたが、『揺れる心に聞こえる』は波に揺られるブイの鐘」と、念仏が聞こえ、三尾の寺の鐘とチャイナハットのブイが同時に鳴り、海は日本とカナダとを分けるものではなく、結ぶものだとわかり、成仏し、時化は止み、白波が消えて海が穏やかになったところで、この能は終わります。

## 企画背景

二〇〇一年春にバンクーバーの劇団、パンゲア・アーツの芸術監督ハイディ・スペクト女史から、カナダ西海岸にいる日系人漁師をテーマにした英語能を作りたいと、突然連絡がきました。氏の希望はカナダ人が作者で、私が作曲、そして松井彬氏にも参加してほしいということでした。バンクーバー日系移民には和歌山県人が多いことをよく知っていたスペクト氏は、松井氏が和歌山市の方で、彼が初めて外国に行ったのは和歌山市の姉妹都市であるバンクーバーの隣のリッチモンド市への文化交流使節団の一員としてだったと私が伝えたとき、たいへん喜び、これこそやらなくてはいけない企画だと決意を固めたのでした。

その夏、スペクト氏は私が毎年指導している米国ペンシルバニア州で行う夏期能実技ワークショプ「能トレーニング・プロジェクト (Noh Training Project)」にも参加して、この話を少しずつ進めました。その後いろいろの連絡を取り合って計画を立てて、ついに二〇〇三年八月、私は初めてバンクーバーに行くことになりました。一週間の能実技ワークショップで教えながら、スペクト氏や彼女が選んだ作者にも会い、次第に企画が具体性を帯びてきました。

4

かもめ

その作者がダフネ・マーラット女史でした。マーラット氏はカナダでは主に詩人として知られ、小説も二冊ほど出版している本格的な作家ですが、今回のように新作英語能はもとより、いわゆる劇作をするのは初めてでした。幸いに本人は前から能に興味を持っていて、一九七〇年代にこのテーマに沿ったスティーブストン村の日系漁師たちに関する詩集も出し、スティーブストンの口頭歴史の本を編集した経験もありました。スペクト氏からはじめて連絡があって、この企画と提案を聞いたとき、すぐ納得してこの新作英語能を書く仕事を引き受けたそうです。

バンクーバーで初めてマーラット氏に会ったとき、印象深いことに、氏の中ではこれから作る能の構造が既によくできていて、ストーリーも私から見るとかなりいい形で、はっきりしていました。能を書きたい数人の外国人にアドバイスを与えた経験のある私にとっては驚きでした。ふつう、劇作家として活躍している人はストーリーと台詞を意識するあまり、一つの作品が能になるためには複雑になりすぎる事が多く、「能」よりも写実的な「劇」になる傾向が多いという気がします。その点、マーラット氏は詩人なので、詩を作るには不要な言葉をカットし、凝縮した表現を心がける仕事に慣れているせいか、能を作るに際しても既にその意識があったようでした。

それから一年間、マーラット氏は「かもめ」を本格的に書き始めました。二〇〇四年八月に企画を次の段階にもっていくため、私は再び二週間ほどバンクーバーに行きました。また実技ワークショップもしましたが、他にスペクトとマーラット両氏と、フェリーで二時間ぐらい離れたガブリオラ島にあるスペクト氏の両親の別荘で、台本を再検討し、作曲に着手し、企画全体の細かい調整をしました。その段階では既に松井氏と私が共同演出をすること特に私の記憶しているのは松井氏の参加でした。その段階では既に松井氏と私が共同演出をすることになっていましたが、スペクト氏は松井氏にシテもやってもらいたいという希望を強く持っていました。ただ、その場合、何語で謡えばいいかという問題がありました。松井さんは、英語ができること

5

はできますが、ご本人にしてみれば英語だけの謡はやりたくないのは明らかでした。そこで気がつい
たのは、シテは和歌山生まれの母の役ですから、英語よりきっと日本語がうまい母で、英語を少し混
じえた日本語で謡ってもらった方が、その母の役としても松井氏自身の役者としてのやりかたでも一
番いいのではないかということです。

その後、マーラット氏は台本の文章を、それが反映するよう
に変えることにしました。あと二つ決めたのは、キャストは男だけにし、そしてこれもスペクト氏の
強い希望でワキ、ワキツレとアイの三人は全部東洋系の役者にすることにしました。

数日後、バンクーバーに戻り、カナダ側のキャストを決めるため、オーディションを行いました。
主としてプロの役者たちがこのオーディションを受け、私、スペクト氏、マーラット氏、そして長く
バンクーバーに滞在し、カナダの劇作品を日本語によく訳していて、今回の「かもめ」の日本語訳も
した吉原豊司氏と、われわれ四人が審査を行いました。受けた役者たちは、パンゲア・アーツの芝居
に出たこともある役者も含め十五人ほどいましたが、私が既に二回指導していたワークショップに一
切参加していない方が多かったことには驚きました。そこで、このオーディションをうまく行うため
に、私は一人々々に能の型を見せ、謡を聞かせ、それを真似てもらって、その上でワキ、ワキツレ、
アイ、そして四人の地謡をキャストとして決めました。

最初のリハーサルは二〇〇五年四月末からの二週間、バンクーバーの郊外にあるバーナビー市の日
系センターで行いました。松井氏は参加したのはこのときからでした。作詞、作曲、そして日本語へ
の翻訳は殆どできていましたが、このリハーサルでその調整も行われました。英語能ですが、日本語
訳は松井氏のためにも、そして後にお願いする囃子方のためにも必要でした。「かもめ」のリハーサ
ルでありましたが、殆どの役者はこれではじめて能の実技を習うので、「かもめ」だけではなく、能
一般の実技ワークショップも行いました。古典の仕舞や謡、囃子の稽古も毎日すこしずつ行いながら、

6

「かもめ」という演目の謡や動きも覚える必要があり、二週のリハーサル期間の最後に「ワーク・イン・プログレス」、いわゆる公演に近い公開リハーサルも二つが計画されていたので、役者は連日大忙しでした。最後の公開リハーサル会場は、日系センターの他に日系人の多くがよく働いていた現在博物館になっているスティーブストン村の、もとサケ漁缶詰工場でした。その意味でもこの公演が成功したことは間違いありません。

本番の二〇〇六年五月の公演のため、四月末からまた松井氏と二人でバンクーバーに出かけ、最終的なリハーサルを行いました。それは主にUBC（ブリティシュコロンビア大学）のシアター科の施設で行い、前もって日本で別のリハーサルをしていた囃子方は、本番の数日前にカナダに着き、初めて全員が顔を合わせました。リッチモンド市役所前に建てられた仮設舞台は、波止場をイメージしたもので、鏡板は老松の替わりにチャイナハットの湾の絵でした。

公演を六回行い、パンゲア・アーツの宣伝も行き届いたためか、殆ど毎日、満員もしくは満員に近い状態でした。事実、評判もたいへん良かったようで、非常に感動した観客が多かったように見受けました。またこの公演は国際演劇協会（International Theatre Institute）によって高く評価され、同協会が日本の伝統的演劇形式の海外普及に資した個人あるいは団体に毎年贈る「内村直也賞」を受賞するに至りました。

この企画は能の専門家とそうでない演者たちのコラボレーションで、日本で見られる新作能とは明らかに違いますが、主要な役であるシテ、囃子、地頭が能の専門家であったため、ちゃんとした力のある新作能として成り立ちました。そして、カナダ西海岸の戦後史を知っている日系人も含むカナダ人はこの能のカナダ風なタッチに深い感動を覚えたのではないでしょうか。それは、能が形式や技法を通じて、日本の古典の能だけではなく、外国の題材でも普遍性を感じさせ、感動を与える力を持っ

7

ているからだと私は思います。

**ダフネ・マーラット Daphne Marlatt ──** バンクーバー在住の国際的に知られる詩人、小説家。二〇〇六年にカナダ国の「オーダー・オブ・カナダ」受賞。小説「アナ・ヒストリク」と「テーケン」、詩集「チス・トレマー・ラーブ・イズ」他十三集や、ノンフィクションも多くある。一九七四年にロバート・ミンドンの写真との詩集「スティーブストン」、一九七六年にスティーブストン口頭歴史集の編集や、一九七七年に「スティーブストン」というラジオドラマなどがある。

**吉原　豊司 ──** 一九六〇年、早稲田大学文学部卒業。一九七〇年、住友商事（株）駐在員としてカナダに渡航。以後カナダに在住し、仕事の傍らカナダ戯曲の邦訳（三十本）、日本戯曲の英訳（四本）、日本・カナダ間の演劇交流促進等に尽力。二〇〇〇年、住友商事退職後、カナダ演劇の対日紹介を目的とする「メープルリーフ・シアター」の創設に参画。二〇〇〇年、カナダ・マクマスター大学名誉文学博士、二〇〇二年、湯浅芳子賞（翻訳脚色部門）受賞。訳書に「カナダ戯曲選集」（全三巻、東京・彩流社刊）他がある。

## 「かもめ」公演記録

二〇〇六年五月十日〜十四日（全六回）カナダ、リッチモンド市、市役所前の仮設テント内にて。

かもめ

作　　　　　　　　　　　ダフネ・マーラット
作曲・演出・音楽監督　　リチャード・エマート
演出・型付け　　　　　　松井　彬
制作・芸術監督　　　　　ハイディ・スペクト
制作補佐　　　　　　　　レナード・スタンガ
舞台美術　　　　　　　　フィリップ・ティード
衣装デザイン　　　　　　マーガレット・マケー
能面制作　　　　　　　　久保博山
鏡板制作　　　　　　　　エリザベス・ヘズルティップ
日本語訳　　　　　　　　吉原豊司
出演　　シテ　　　　　　松井　彬
　　　　ワキ　　　　　　サイモン・ハヤマ
　　　　ワキツレ　　　　アルビン・カタクタン
　　　　アイ狂言　　　　デビッド・フジノ
　　　　地頭　　　　　　リチャード・エマート
　　　　地謡　　　　　　アリ・サロモン／マイケル・ロビンソン／山本　稔／
　　　　　　　　　　　　ケリー・バンデルグラインド
笛　　　　　　　　　　　滝沢成美
小鼓　　　　　　　　　　高橋奈王子
大鼓　　　　　　　　　　釜　三夫

太鼓　　　　　　　　　桜井　均

後見　　　　　　　　　平野弥生

技術監督　　　　　　　ビル・デイビー

舞台制作　　　　　　　テリース・ハートウイグ

舞台制作　　　　　　　デーブ・アレン

舞台制作補佐　　　　　ジュディ・ハレブスキー

劇場コーディネーター　イボンヌ・イップ

舞台監督　　　　　　　クリステン・アイベルセン

舞台助監督　　　　　　アケミ・コモリ

衣装付け　　　　　　　トニー・ハドクラフト

衣装制作　　　　　　　イダ・ショウコ

着物制作　　　　　　　マリアム・アスガリ

衣装制作　　　　　　　山城猛夫

通訳　　　　　　　　　レナ・タバタ

リハーサル通訳　　　　ハンズ・セフコウ

ポスター　　　　　　　アニカ・ランジェルー

プログラム

※この記事は東京の武蔵野大学能楽資料センター紀要（No.18　二〇〇六年）の翻刻です。

# 登場人物

マエジテ（一幕目のシテ）　若い日系一世の女／かもめ。
淡い色合いのキモノの上に灰色の蓑を着、若い女の面をかぶる。

ノチジテ（二幕目のシテ）　日系一世の女。中年。
伝統的なワカヤマ風のキモノ。中年女の面をかぶる。

ワキ　日系二世の漁師。二十才代の終り。
一九五〇年代カナダ西海岸の漁師の衣裳。

ワキツレ　ワキの弟。
ワキと同じような衣裳。

アイキョウゲン　五十才代終りの漁師。
ワキと同じく、一九五〇年代カナダ西海岸の漁師の衣裳。

ジ（地）　六人の謡い手。男性。

楽師たち　袴に黒衣。
大鼓、小鼓、太鼓、能管。
いずれも伝統衣裳を着ている。

11

# 第一幕 （前場<ruby>マエバ</ruby>）

## 第一景

シダイ（次第＝導入楽）ワキとワキツレが橋懸りから本舞台へ進み出る。一人はランタンを持ち、一人は魚網を肩に負い、鉤棹<ruby>かぎざお</ruby>を手に持っている。

**シダイ**

ワキ・ワキツレ　（本舞台に至り、正面を向く）
晩い春、濡れそぼる海霧<ruby>うみぎり</ruby>の中、我は帰る、ついに帰る
晩い春、濡れそぼる海霧の中、我は帰る、ついに帰る
父の馴染みし、この漁場<ruby>ぎょば</ruby>に
荒れ狂う、海のしぶき

ジトリ（地取）
晩い春、濡れそぼる海霧の中、我は帰る、ついに帰る

父の馴染みし、この漁場に
荒れ狂う、海のしぶき

ワキ

**（名ノリ）** ワキとワキツレ、舞台中央に立ち正面を向く。

われら、スティーブストンより海へ漕ぎ出す日系の漁師。戦争終りて五年、生まれ育ちしこの海辺を追われて八年。ようようにして漁に戻ることが許された。缶詰工場に雇われて漁をすることにはなりしものの、父親の持ち船は最早なく、この船は借り物。両親は共に亡くなった。全財産を没収され、売り払われ、山奥への疎開を強いられた挙句に。だが、われら兄弟は帰って来た。そして、海岸線を遡る、スキーナの早瀬を目指し、借り物の船で。

**（道行）** ワキとワキツレ、舞台ソデに面する。

ワキ・ワキツレ

漕ぎ上りつつ思い出す
セーモアー海峡、リップル・ロック
潮の流れや、目印の岩

**ウチキリ**（短い器楽の間奏）

13

ワキツレ　　セーモアー海峡、リップル・ロック
　　　　　　潮の流れや、目印の岩
　　　　　　円いブイやら、鈴付きのブイ
　　　　　　白く連なる波頭（なみがしら）
　　　　　　やがて見えるはジョンソンの瀬戸
　　　　　　シャチが群れては飛び上がり
　　　　　　戻りしわれらに、挨拶をする

ワキ・ワキツレ　　　　**ウチキリ**

　　　　　　山奥に
　　　　　　閉じ込められし、このわが身
　　　　　　二度と乗ることあるまじと
　　　　　　思いし船に、今また乗って
　　　　　　しっかり握るは艫（とも）の舵
　　　　　　うねりにうねり、揺れる船
　　　　　　イルカのごとき波頭（なみがしら）
　　　　　　北へ登ってクイーン・シャーロット海峡
　　　　　　ミルバンクから、スインドルの入江へ
　　　　　　風を欺き、北上す

ワキ　（正面を向いて）

暮れ行く太陽、最期の光
黒く浮かぶは岩の鋒
夕日に佇む岩の峯

ツキゼリフ　（着キゼリフ）

そして、われらは着いた。懐かしのチャイナ・ハットに。岩だらけの入江は、迫り来る嵐からの避難所(ひなんどころ)。スティーブストンから来た他の船と並び、われらも舫う、夜の嵐をやり過ごすために。この小さな入江に帰り来しわれら、まるで里帰りした鮭のごとし。

第二景

イッセイ（一声）マエジテの導入楽。かもめ女に扮したシテが橋懸りから登場。灰色の蓑の下に淡色のキモノ。若い女の面をつけている。

**イッセイ**

シテ　（日本語で）時代（ときよ）の波の悪戯（いたずら）に
　　　居場所定めぬ迷い鳥
　　　我が家と呼べる家もなく
　　　荒波避ける苫（とま）もなし

**サシ**

シテ　（日本語で）より良い暮らしの約束に
　　　誘われ一人来たれるも

ジ　（地）が謡う間に、シテは橋懸かりに佇む。

ジ

　運命（さだめ）の風に航路を外（はず）し
　故郷（くに）を離れて夢追うた、それが、このわれ、迷い鳥
　至りしところは大河口（だいかこう）

ジ

**ウタ**（現代詩、註①）

　われらはつとに言ったもの
　子供と海と太陽が、あまねくこの世を満ちみたす
　網と漁船とキンセンカ
　それらに満ちた我が家のごとく
　夢中（むちゅう）に立つは、彼の地の我が家

**ジョウのエイ（上の詠）**

シテ　（日本語で）荒波に、怒りが我が身を追い立てる
　　　打ちひしがれし迷い鳥

ジ

シテ、袖で顔を隠し、橋懸かりに座る。

吹き寄せられし、この地では
過酷な運命の波風に
問わるれば応えもしよう、このわれに、いささかもなし、安らぎは

## 第三景

### モンドウ（問答）

ワキ　（ワキツレと共に立ち上がって）
この雨の中、桟橋で喋っているのは何者だろう？

ワキツレ　私には聞こえませぬ。かもめが鳴いているのでは？

ワキ　女のように聞こえる。だが、このインディアン部落で、誰が日本語を話すというのだ。（シテに向かって）失礼だが、そこの方、私どもに話し掛けておられるのかな？

　　　　シテ、顔を背ける。

ワキツレ　おかしな鳥だ。翼に頭を埋めたりして。

ワキ　判らぬか、あれは女だ。袖で顔を隠しおる。私らに驚いたのだろう。

ワキツレ　（ランタンを持ち上げて）良く見えぬ。この暗さと、この雨で。女であれ、かもめであれ、言葉が通じるかどうか、試してみよう……もしもし、こんばんわ。私らに、あなたを驚かすつもりはない。どちらから、おいでかな？

シテ　（頭を上げ、ゆっくりと振り返って、ワキと向かい合う。そして、日英両語を混ぜて謡い語る）

　　　　渡りの鳥は行く、戻る。されど、ホームは紀伊のミオ……

ワキ　（シテに）

　　　　ミオとな？　ワカヤマのミオ？　ミオならばわが母親の郷里（ふるさと）……わが母親の村だ。

シテ　（英語まじりの日本語で、兄弟に謡い語る）

　　　　荒波に、打ち上げられし、我が身には、ノー・チャイルド、ノー・ハズバンド、ノー・

　　　　ファーザー、ノー・マザー。

ワキ　（ワキツレに）

　　　　何と言っているのだ？

ワキツレ　（ワキツレに）

　　　　このものの喋り方を聞いていると、わが母の話を聞いているようだ。日本語は少し

　　　　しか解らぬが、どうやら、家族もなく、なぜかこの地に迷い込んだと言っているら

　　　　しい。

シテ　（二人から離れ、日本語で語る）

　　　　心は羽ばたく、かもめのごとく。されどこの身は動きも取れず。

ワキ　（シテに）

　　　　私ら二人はこの海辺に生まれた。父親は私らを学校に入れてくれたが、それは英

　　　　語の学校。日本語は覚束ないが、ご容赦くだされ。

シテ　（再び二人の方を向き、日本語で語る）

　　　　異国の浜の水辺に浮かぶ、打ちひしがれしミオの鳥。

　　　　ワカヤマからおいでの若い女人（にょにん）。そのあなたが、なぜ、この遠い入江に？

ワキ　　このインディアン部落に？

20

シテ　(元うたを日本語で謡う)
　　　われもまた、いざ、こと問わん、ミヤコドリ……　(註②)
　　　(ホームという言葉以外は日本語で)　主らの知らぬ古の、物語から引くこの言葉。

ワキ　哀れなミオのかもめには、ホームというものあらざりし。
　　　ホームですと?　鮭の海、ここそが私らのホーム。われわれ漁師は自由の身となっ

シテ　(大部分を日本語で)
　　　て、ここに帰ってこられたことを、とても喜んでいる。
　　　この地におらば、何事が、主らを待つか見えざるや?
　　　主らも同じミオ・バード。風のまにまにコースを外し、異国に漂うミオ・バード。

ジ　　　　　　ウタ　(現代詩から、註③)

　　　桟橋の灯かりに影が伸び縮む
　　　前に後ろに、長く短く
　　　話す言葉に似合わぬ我が顔
　　　絶えず数える、自由の日々を
　　　重く貴重な自由の日々を

　　　この岸に、かつてはありし自由の日
　　　古い昔の物語

モンドウ

ワキ　（ワキツレに）

不思議だ。この女のする話には、聞き覚えがある。

ツレ　と言うと？

ワキ　故郷のミオを恋しがり、私らの母親も同じようなことを言っていた。

ツレ　戦争が終り、故郷に戻りたいと言っていた、あの頃に？

ワキ　いや、その前からだ。まだ幼かったお前は、覚えておらぬだろうが。

ワキツレ、座る。

ワキ、舞台中央へ進み出る。

第四景

　　　クリ

ジ（ワキのために謡う）
　　その昔、若妻、海を越えきたり
　　ミオの釣り船、父母の家、
　　竜王神社を後にして
　　神戸の港に別れをば告げ

　　　サシ

ジ
　　ヒノミサキを通り過ぎ
　　潮に袖を打ち濡らし
ワキ
　　ふるさとを背に見詰めるは
　　手中に握る小さな写真
　　未来の夫の小さな写真

ワキ　若く、締まった、その身体

ジ　頼るは手紙のその言葉——
　魚満ちたる大河口
　そこに佇む新しき村
　無限に続く広大な空

ワキ　そこに待つのは輝く未来

シテ（日本語で）われは見た、輝く未来を、眼前に

　シテ、蓑を捨て、立上がる。

ジ　若妻は見たり、眼前に輝く将来を

**クセ**

　シテ、橋懸かりで立ち上がり、翼を広げる。本舞台に進み出て、ゆっくりと舞い始め、やがて以下の台詞に合わせて動きを早める。

ジ　だが、着いてみると、全ては一場の夢
　男は写真よりも年をとっており
　荒れた河口に立つのは、冬の風が薄い壁を吹きぬける

シテ

（日本語で）

　　肺病やみたちの小屋
　　ストライキに赤ん坊
　　船を、網（あみ）を、そして家を持つために繰り返す
　　際限のない借金

**ウチキリ**

　　詰（なじ）られ、脅かされ、
　　挙句にやって来たのが戦争
　　全てが没収され、売り払われた
　　苦労の末に手に入れた漁船も家もクルマまで
　　「敵性民族」の烙印を押され、囲い込まれた我々を
　　扶養する為と称して
　　家族は引き裂かれ、海辺から追放された
　　凍てつく山奥の収容所に
　　ゴーストタウンの掘建て小屋に
　　ぎゅうぎゅう詰めの掘建て小屋に

ジ

　　　怒りが焦がす、この翼
　　　何ともひどい騙まし討ち

ジ

チャイナ・ハットに逆巻く嵐
波頭（はとう）に砕ける女の叫び

地謡の続く中、シテは橋懸かりに戻り、ワキ、ワキツレの方に向き直る。
飛ぶかのように二人に近付き、身を翻して、また橋懸かりに戻る。

ジ

不思議なり。この女の語る物語、わが母親のそれにそっくり
――「待て」、漁師は叫ぶ、「そなたは何者？」
女は、長旅にささくれ、そぼ濡れた翼をはばたく
あとに残るは、虚空を切り裂くかもめの鳴き声――
愚かにも、ミオから来たりし渡り鳥、
帰るが良いぞ、故郷（ふるさと）へ！

最後の台詞に合わせ、シテは跪き片翼を上げる。
鋭い能管のソロ。
シテ、立ち上がり、素早く退場。

風の蜃気楼、怒りの雨
残るは女にあらずして、一羽のかもめ、逸（はぐ）れたかもめ
……だが何と、口をききたり、そのかもめ

26

# 幕間狂言

アイキョウゲン　（民謡「串本節」の一番を歌いながら、橋懸りに登場）

　　ヒノの岬に、灯台あぁれど

　　恋の闇路は照らしゃせぇえぬ

　　アラ、よいしょ、よーいしょ、よいしょ、よーいしょ

アイキョウゲン　（シテの定位置で）

　私は日系の漁師。かつてはスティーヴストンを足場にしていたが、やがてカスローの山奥へ——漁などは、思いもよらぬ山奥の日系人強制収容所へ。去年になってやっと海辺に戻ることが出来た。規制が外れ、最初に戻ってきた一人だ。今年は、このチャイナ・ハットに舫う仲間が一段と増えた。（ワキとワキツレの方を向いて）ほれ、新手がもう一組み……やあ、やあ、どうやら間に合ったようじゃな！おや、誰かが桟橋から呼んでいる。年老いた漁師のようだ。

ワキ　（ワキツレと一緒に立ち上がり）

ワキツレ

アイ　（二人のほうに歩み寄る）よお、そこの方！　嵐がやって来る。こちらにおいでなされ！

ワキ　生憎だねえ、この嵐！　だが、日系の漁師がどんどん海に戻ってくるのは嬉しい。

アイ　抜かりはないだろうが、しっかり舫いで、気をつけていた方がいい。ところで、そちらは誰に雇われて？

ワキ　ネルソン・ブラザーズに。

アイ　ということは、あなた方はアラカワさんの息子たちかな？

ワキ　ご存知ですか、私たちの父を？

アイ　知ってるとも！　お父上とはスキーナで永年一緒に漁をした。最後は一九四一年の夏。あの時は息子さんを連れていなさった。あれは、あなただったのでは？　私はハリー・タカハシという者です。

ワキ　タカハシさん！　九年のご無沙汰。お見逸れしました。

アイ　様々な出来事があったからね。この海は昔と同じだが、わたしらは変わった。わしはお父上とロッキーの道路作りキャンプで一緒だったが、やがて別のところに移された。そこでだよ、お父上が事故に会われたことを聞いたのは。腕の立つ漁師だった。息子さん二人が、こうしてこの海に戻り、漁をしているのをご覧になったら、さぞ喜ばれただろうに。

ワキ　久し振りにお目に掛かれて、嬉しく存じます。お祝いといきましょう。

アイ　うむ、この雨の中、ウイスキーの一献は、きっと身体を温（ぬく）めてくれる。

ワキツレ　まずはお掛けください。（アイキョウゲンに椅子を用意する）さあ、どうぞ、どうぞ。

アイ　（酒瓶を持ってくる。アイとワキ、扇を広げる。ツレ、それに酒を注ぐ仕草）乾杯。（一同、杯を干す）ああ、旨い！　だが、長居は出来ぬ。風が出てきた。で、お母上はいかが？

鋭い鼓の音。
大波に船が揺れる。

ワキツレ　（よろめき）ヤレヤレ、今のは大きかった！

ワキ　（アイと一緒にこちらも身体を揺らし）戦争が終って　間もなく、母も肺病で亡くなりました。ニュー・デンバーのサナトリュームで。

アイ　それはお気の毒に。ご両親を共に亡くされたとは。

ワキ　母の最後は、とても不幸せなものでした。政府のいう「本国送還（オカミ）」に応じ、一家揃って日本へ帰ることを、しきりに望んでおりました。ここはもう沢山、ミオへ帰りたいというのが口癖で。

アイ　（首を振り）

アイ　あの、お母上がねえ。（扇を傾け、杯が空であることを示す）

ワキツレ　さあ、もう一杯、いかがです。（アイ、杯を差し出す。ツレ、それに酒を注ぐ）

アイ　ああ、旨い！（舌鼓を打つ）お母上は格別のお方だった。古くゆかしいワカヤマ人

29

ワキツレ （また寄せてきた大波に三人、大きく揺れる）
　　　　いかん、益々荒れてきた！

　　　　　　　　　　鋭い鼓の音。

アイ　　ひどいシケになりそうだ。かもめが、飛沫を上げて波間を飛び回っていた。大嵐の
　　　　兆しだよ。

ワキ　　あなたも見ましたか、あのかもめを。

ワキツレ あなたがおいでになるちょっと前、私らも、かもめが桟橋で喋っているのを聞きま
　　　　した。まるで私らを叱りつけるように。

アイ　　かもめはみんな、そんな風に鳴くものだ。山の暮らしが長くなって、お忘れかな？

ワキ　　（扇を差し出し、酒のお代りを求める。ツレ、それに酒を注ぐ）
　　　　あれは、ただのかもめじゃありませんでしたよ、タカハシさん。口をきいたんです。
　　　　そんな馬鹿なとおっしゃるでしょうが、日本語で。私らに故郷へ帰れと言うんです。

アイ　　（苦笑して）
　　　　かもめまでが故郷へ帰れとな？

　　　　　　　　　　鋭い鼓の音。

30

ワキ・アイ・ツレ　（三人、また大波に揺れる）
　　　　　　　　ワーオ！

ワキ　　というよりも、私たちは間違った所に来ていると言いたげでした。

アイ　　ふむ、そうか。ひょっとすると、おまえさん方が見たのは、かもめじゃないかも知
　　　　れぬ。チャイナ・ハットには伝説があってのお。船に幽霊が現れるのを見たという
　　　　者が何人もおる。

　　　　　　　　ワキとワキツレ、顔を見合わせる。

ワキ　　まさか……（アイに）我々の母親について、まだ、何か？

アイ　　あの人が初めてスティーヴストンに着いた時のことは、よく覚えている。「この野郎、
　　　　若いころの写真をミオに送って、うまいことやりやがって」と、わしはあんたがた
　　　　のお父さんが羨ましかった。もっとも、その頃は、誰もがそうしていた本当の
　　　　年令が判ったんじゃ、若い娘が遥々海を越えて来てくれるかどうか、自信がなかっ
　　　　たからね。お母上はお父さんより十五歳年下で、ミオのお寺の娘さんだった。学問
　　　　もあるし、器量もいい。もっと良い相手はいくらでもいたはずだ。だが、冒険心に
　　　　富んだお方でな。世界を見たかったんだろう。ところが、来てみると、スティーヴ
　　　　ストンは期待していたようなところじゃなかった。洪水になる度に「何という荒れ
　　　　ようでしょう、ここの河は」と、そう言っていなさった。火事に洪水、掘建て小屋
　　　　の缶詰め工場、桟橋のはずれにあるたった一つの水道の蛇口。こぼしちゃいたが、

ワキ　よく働く人だった。お前さんたちを育てながら、近所の女房どもと一緒に缶詰め工場で働いていなさった。でも、心の中じゃ、もっと良い暮らしも出来たのにと、夢想してたに違いない。お前さんがたの親父さんが、いつだったか言っていたよ。「一儲けしたら、必ずワカヤマに帰ると、カミさんに約束させられた」ってな。だが、親父さんはこの土地が好きだった。だから、儲けた金は船に化け、家に化け、二隻目の新しい船に化けちまった。漁師稼業は益々しんどくなる。その挙句におっぱじまったのが戦争。

アイ　そう、戦争……辛い時代でした。

ワキ　おまえさんがたはまだ子供だった。オーチャードへ送られたんだろう、母上と一緒に？

ワキツレ　最初はグリーンウッドでした。スティーブストンの他の家族と一緒に。

ワキ　店仕舞いしていた古いホテルに押し込められました。何世帯もがぎゅうぎゅう詰めで、台所はたったの一つ。

アイ　それでも幸運だった方。あとで聴いた話では、ポポフに送られた仲間など、最初の冬はテント暮らし。朝方なんぞ、毛布に霜が降っていたとのことでした。

ワキ　その通り。わしらも道路キャンプからスローカンに移され、収容所の小屋づくりをさせられた。冬が来るというのに、造っても造っても間に合わぬ始末。

ワキツレ　日本から慰問袋が届いた冬を覚えています。煎茶が入っていて、母がお茶を淹れました。いつまでもなくならないようにと、ちびりちびりと飲んでいました。これこそ故郷(くに)の味だといいながら。

32

かもめ

アイ　うむ、煎茶か！　煎茶に勝る美味はない。ウイスキーは別にしてな　……（アイ、
　　　ツレに目配せを送る。ツレはもう一杯、注ぐ。ワキは遠慮）

アイ（厳粛に）その頃です、母がひどく咳き込み始めたのは。

ワキツレ　うむ、わしも思い出した、お母上の空咳を！
ワキ　グリーンウッドで悪くなりました。最後には咳に血が混じって。
ワキ　その時です、オーチャードに移されたのは。仲間の中には砂糖大根の農場に移るも
　　　のもいました。そっちのほうが混んでおらず、幾分ゆったりとしていたので。
ワキ　やがて「本国送還」の命令がでました。母は、われわれミオに帰るべきだといって
　　　いました。父が道路工事のキャンプで亡くなり、先の暮らしが心配だったからでしょ
　　　う。

ワキツレ　でも、私らが働く、森林伐採のキャンプに行けば仕事はいくらでもある、と私ら
は　言い張りました。
ワキ　いずれにしろ、あの容態では、旅どころではありませんでした。
ワキツレ　カナダは私らを欲しがっていない、それが母の口癖でした。
アイ　そう言う白人が多かったからの。知っておるだろうが。
ワキ　しかし、タカハシさん、私らはここで生まれ、日本語も話せない。スティーヴスト
　　　ンこそが私らの故郷です。
アイ　おまえさんがたは難しい世代にいる。日本人でもなく、かといってカナダ人でもな
　　　く　……
　　　　お母上はサナトリウムで亡くなられたとのことだったな？

33

ワキ　はい。私らは樵の仕事で山に入ってました。知らせを聞き、大急ぎで戻ってみると、母はカーテンの引かれたベッドに横たわっていました。ゼイゼイと苦しそうな息遣いで、海を、そして風を恋求めながら……

鋭い鼓。

ワキ・アイ・ツレ　（大きなうねりに椅子から転げ落ちそうになり）ワーオ！

アイ　いよいよ荒れてきた。船に戻るとしよう。（下手に行き、戸外を窺う。振り向いて）不思議だ。外は晴れあがって来た。そんなには荒れていない。

ワキ　じゃ、この揺れは波の所為じゃないとでも？

アイ　うむ。何か他に理由がありそうだ。（間）お前さん方が見たというかもめは、ひょっとすると、悶え苦しむお母上の霊魂かも知れぬ。

ワキツレ　どうして私らがここにいるとわかったんでしょう、その母親の霊魂とやらは？

アイ　チャイナ・ハットは不思議な場所でな。行き場の無い死人の魂がここに集まってくるとか。

ワキ　どうしたらいいんだ。

アイ　二人でデッキに出ていなさい。お母上はお前さん方に何かを話したがっているのだろう、きっと。

ワキ　（独り言のように）

34

本当に母親だろうか？　（アイに向かって）　我々は起きていて、様子を見ます。
お手助け、有難うございました。

　アイ、ゆっくりと橋懸りに向かう。途中で立ち止まり、空を見上げ、かも
めを探すかのように海面を見やる。やがて自分を見詰めているワキとワキ
ツレを振り返り、頷く。
　二人は恭しくお辞儀を返す。
　アイは呟くように、歌の続きを歌いながら、橋懸りを退場。

# 第二幕　（後場<sub>ノチバ</sub>）

## 第一景

### マチウタイ（待謡）

ワキ／ワキツレ　（座って）

　収まりゆく嵐
　古い毛布に身を包み
　われら舳先<sub>へさき</sub>にまどろむ

### ウチキリ

　収まりゆく嵐
　われら舳先にまどろむ

かもめ

そして待つ
二つの世界の狭間にあり
わが船と
漁場に帰らんとするわが志を揺する
心休まぬ霊魂が、また現れぬかと
仮令夢の中にでも

第二景

デハ（出端）の音楽。シテが中年の女の姿で橋懸りに現れる。

**イッセイ／サシ**

シテ（日本語で）　生死（いきしに）の狭間さまよう、この我が身
嵐に騒ぐ波の間（ま）に
映る姿は迷い鳥

　　　　シテ、橋懸かりを経て、シテバシラ（シテ柱）に至る。

ジ　　とこ永遠（とわ）に、飛ぶは宿命（さだめ）の暗い海
この地に住まう我が子らに
掛けるその声、いと哀し
砕ける波に、いと哀し

第三景

カケアイ（掛ケ合）

ワキ　（立ち上がる）　そこなるデッキに、例のかもめがとまりおる。雲間からさす朧な月明かりに照らされて。

ワキツレ　（同じく立ち上がる）　慌しく動く雲の晴れ間に、白々と浮かび上がるその姿。あれは、わが母であろうか？

シテ　（マイ・サンズ "My Sons" の二語は英語で、それ以外は日本語で）　マイ・サンズ、住まい失い行き惑う、この我が身をば、誰と思う？

ワキ　（ワキツレに）　あの姿、この世のものとは思えぬ。

シテ　いかにも、この身は、暗い海。

ワキツレ　本当に、おわしますのか、ここの地に？

ワキツレ、シテに近付こうとする。ワキ、両手を広げ、押し留める。

シテ　（日本語で）　そなたたちとは、別の海。

ワキ　（ワキツレに）　別の海？

シテ　（啜り泣きの仕草で身を翻し、英語の混じった日本語で）
　　　ミオよ、ミオ、失われたる我が故郷。失われたる我がホーム。

ジ　　**ダンウタ（段歌）** シテ、ジの謡に合わせて「マイム・ダンス」を舞う

　　　果てしなき海の彼岸
　　　香しき白砂の松に
　　　潮うちよせるキイ（紀伊）
　　　浜に干す古（いにしえ）からのシラス網
　　　われ、父親の寺にて綱を引き、鈴を鳴らす
　　　そして唱える阿弥陀の名
　　　南無阿弥陀仏、阿弥陀仏
　　　波頭を越え
　　　迷えるものを西の楽土に導く阿弥陀仏
　　　われをミオへ引き戻す鈴の綱、郷愁の絆
　　　その痛みを断ち切りうるは、ひとり阿弥陀仏のみ
　　　われをミオに引き戻さんとするこの絆、この痛み

かもめ

## カケアイ （不揃いに歌われる）

ワキ　（ワキツレと立ち上がりながら）
　　　だが、そのミオも
　　　戦争の嵐で様変わり
　　　我とわが身が変わりしょうに

　　　　　　　　　シテ、橋懸かりに向かう。

ジ　　　嵐にしかと、捉えられ
　　　自ら作りし郷愁の
　　　哀れなるかな迷い鳥

シテ　（橋懸かりから）
　　　そなた達、この身が生みし息子達
ジ　　　息子達、この身が生みし息子達 ─

41

ワキ　　そなた達には解からぬか
　　　　何が心に掛かるかを
　　　　それは故郷（ふるさと）、わが生家

ワキツレ　お母上、
　　　　あなたの嘆きは、わが嘆き
　　　　とは言え、時世（ときょ）の移ろいに
　　　　変わらぬものなど、あるまじき

シテ　　この地にありても移ろいの、波は激しく
　　　　ご覧の通り
　　　　この我々にも襲いかかる

ジ　　　（身を翻して）
　　　　我が身に絡むこの絆、昔をしのぶこの絆
　　　　苦き思いのこの絆
　　　　さまよう我の魂を
　　　　いまだに、きつく絡めとる

　　　　　イロエ

シテ、曲の間、舞台を一回りし、二人の息子の前に来てとまる。二人を責め立てるかのように。

# エイ（詠）

シテ（英語で）　「ユー・レット・ミー・ダイ」（"You let me die"）

ジ　　　　　　　山の奥なる病院に
　　　　　　　　閉じ込められし、この我が身
　　　　　　　　それをば運ぶ海風も、
　　　　　　　　ここには吹かず、里遠し

ワキ　　　　　　母上が、かの地でしのびし心の痛み
　　　　　　　　いかに淋しくおられたか

ワキ／ツレ　　　それを解さぬは不肖の息子
シテ　　　　　　お許しください、われらの不明
（日本語と英語で）

ワキ　　　　　　帰れホームへ、そなたらも。
　　　　　　　　なれど母上、母上のホームは、最早、我々のホームではありませぬ。

ジ　　　　　　　ホーム、それは変わる
　　　　　　　　漕ぎ出す海の荒波のごとく

　　　　　　　　　シテ、ジが謡う中、絶望の態で身を遠ざける。

絶えず変わる
我が移ろいの人生のごとく…

ワキとワキツレ、謡いにつれて舞台を一巡する苦悩のシテを、座って見詰める。

第五景

ノリジ（ノリ地）

ジ　返に窮し、辺り見回す鳥女〔とりおんな〕
　　荒波？　移ろい？　…何を言うのか、この子らは？
　　子らの言葉を解かろうと、努むるものの、いま一つ

ジ　口の端に登るは、唯々、言葉のみ
　　海の息吹に詩人が書くは
　　塩気に重い海の風　（註④）
　　海の潮風、心の息吹
　　素早く遥かに吹き渡る

キリ　シテ、ハヤマイ（早舞）を舞う。

シテ　海の息吹を歌う海
　　　海の息吹を歌う海
　　　寄せてはかえす言葉の潮
　　　悩み乱れる心の中で
　　　「此岸」と「彼岸」を隔てる線も
　　　寄せくる波に跡形もなし

ジ　（此方、彼方を振り向いて）

シテ　カナダの岸か、キイ（紀伊）の浜
　　　彼の地の村か、ワカヤマの
　　　此の地カナダの海辺か

ジ　揺れる心に聞こえるは
　　　波に揺られるブイの鐘
　　　お寺の鐘に聞き紛い
　　　かえりみたれば、そこなるは
　　　二つの浜を繋ぐ海
　　　海原越えて結ばれし
　　　彼の地、此の地の二つ浜
　　　渦巻く潮に結ばれて

46

ジ

隔て消えたる一つ浜

シテ、立ち止まり、聴きいるポーズ。

嵐おさまり、凪ぎのなか
かそけく聞こえる「阿弥陀仏」
波間に聞こえる、その声は
チャイナ・ハットか、ヒノミサキ
南無阿弥陀仏、阿弥陀仏
虚しき波に加わるは
ふと漏れいずる人の息
閃（ひらめ）く悟りに身を放たれて
飛び去るかもめ、ただ一羽

シテ、向きを変えて兄弟を見る。やがて、両手を掲げて橋懸かりに向かい、退場。その後ろ姿に、幕が静かに降りる。

ワキ、ウタイの続く中、舞台前方に立って、かもめの消えていった方角を見詰める。

入り江に光る朝焼けに
悩み解かれしその心
至福の海は波静か
最後に呟く漣も
果てなく続くその海を
乱すことなく波静か
果てなく続くその海を
乱すことなく波静か

# 出典

マエバ（第一幕）

註① ロイ・ミキ作 "Saving Face"（1991）中の「三世の詩」（"Sansei Poem"）から

註② 世阿弥作「隅田川」（Royall Tyler 訳 "Japanese Noh Dramas" 1992）から

註③ ジョイ・コガワ作 "Jericho Road"（1977）中の「オープン・マリッジ」（"Open Marriage"）から

ノチバ（第二幕）

註③ ロイ・キヨオカ作「太平洋の窓」（"Pacific Windows" 1997, ed. Roy Kiooka）中の "Wheels" から

台詞は全てダフネ・マーラット（作曲者リチャード・エマートの助言を得て）

**Above**: Akira Matsui dancing in Act II. *Photo by Hakusan Kubo.*

**Top**: David Fujino (*ai-kyōgen*) looking back at the two brothers from the bridgeway.
**Bottom**: Akira Matsui as *nochijite* (Act II *shite*, the mother's ghost as older woman) descending the bridgeway, beginning of Act II.                     *Photos by Michael Ford.*

**Top**: Akira Matsui as *maejite*, the gull-woman.
**Bottom**: David Fujino as *ai-kyōgen*, with Alvin Catacutan (*wakitsure*) pouring him another drink in the Kyōgen Interlude. *Photos by Michael Ford.*